PEAK DISTRICT WALKS

starting from train stations

© Peter Naldrett, 2013

All Rights Reserved. No part of this publication may be reproduced, stored in a retrieval system, or transmitted in any form or by any means - electronic, mechanical, photocopying, recording, or otherwise - without prior written permission from the publisher or a licence permitting restricted copying issued by the Copyright Licensing Agency, 90 Tottenham Court Road, London W1P 0LA. This book may not be lent, resold, hired out or otherwise disposed of by trade in any form of binding or cover other than that in which it is published, without the prior consent of the publisher.

Moral Rights: The author has asserted his moral right to be identified as the Author of this Work.

Published by Sigma Leisure - an imprint of
Sigma Press, Stobart House, Pontyclerc, Penybanc Road, Ammanford, Carmarthenshire SA18 3HP.

British Library Cataloguing in Publication Data
A CIP record for this book is available from the British Library.

ISBN: 978-1-85058-966-2

Typesetting and Design by: Sigma Press, Ammanford.

Cover photograph: Headstone Viaduct from Monsal Head © Peter Naldrett

Photographs: © Peter Naldrett unless stated otherwise.

Every effort has been made to fulfil requirements with regard to reproducing copyright material. The author and publisher will be glad to rectify any ommissions at the earliest opportunity

Maps: Rebecca Terry

Printed by: TJ International, Padstow, Cornwall

Disclaimer: the information in this book is given in good faith and is believed to be correct at the time of publication. No responsibility is accepted by either the author or publisher for errors or omissions, or for any loss or injury however caused. Only you can judge your own fitness, competence and experience. Do not rely solely on sketch maps for navigation: we strongly recommend the use of appropriate Ordnance Survey (or equivalent) maps.

PEAK DISTRICT WALKS

starting from train stations

Peter Naldrett

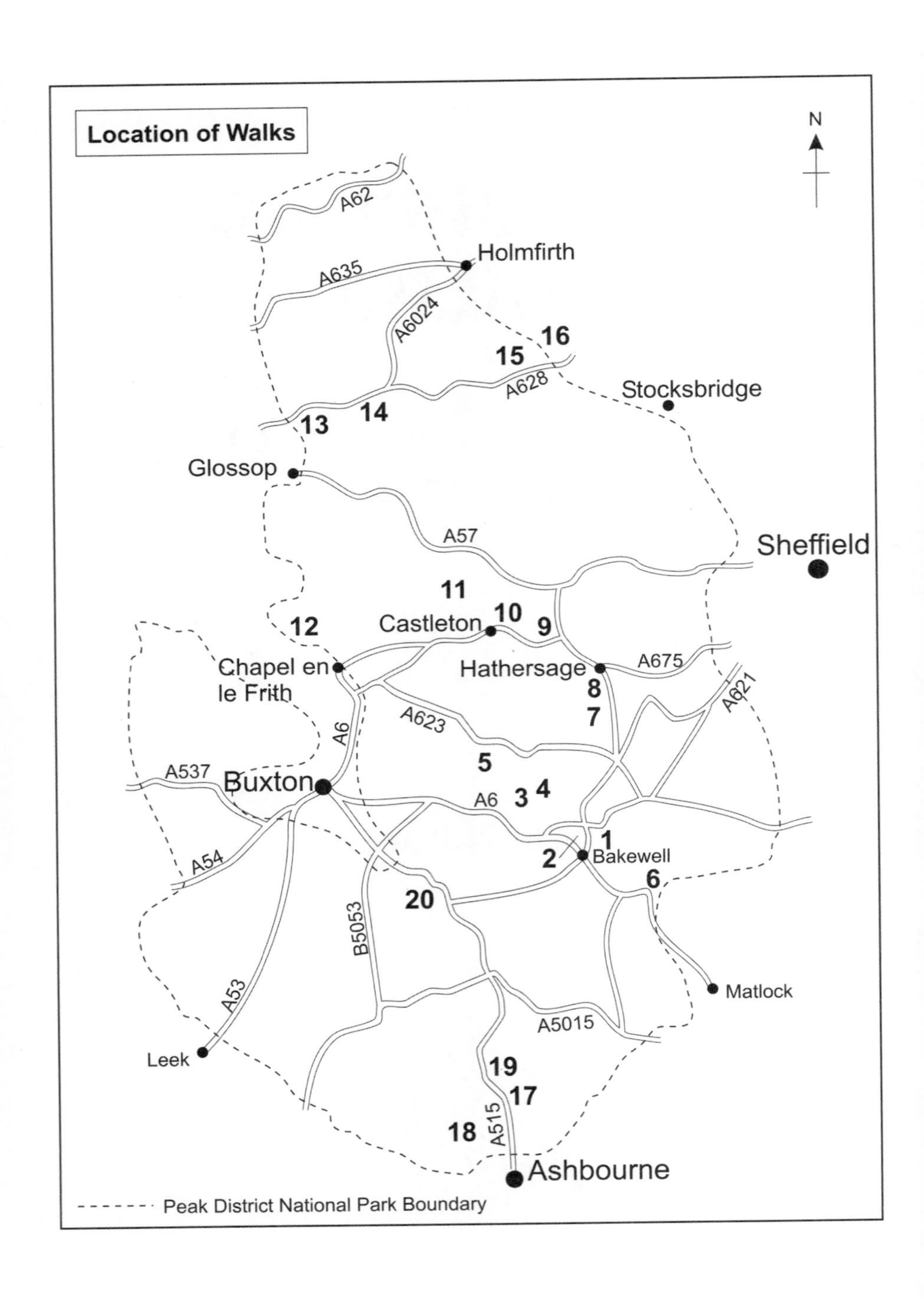
Location of Walks
N
A62
Holmfirth
A635
A6024
16
15
A628
Stocksbridge
14
13
Glossop
A57
Sheffield
11
10
Castleton
9
12
Chapel en le Frith
Hathersage
A675
8
7
A621
A623
A6
5
A537
Buxton
4
3
A6
1
2
Bakewell
A54
6
20
B5053
Matlock
A53
A5015
Leek
19
17
18
A515
Ashbourne
Peak District National Park Boundary

Contents

For Nicola, Toby and Willow, who joined me on the walks.

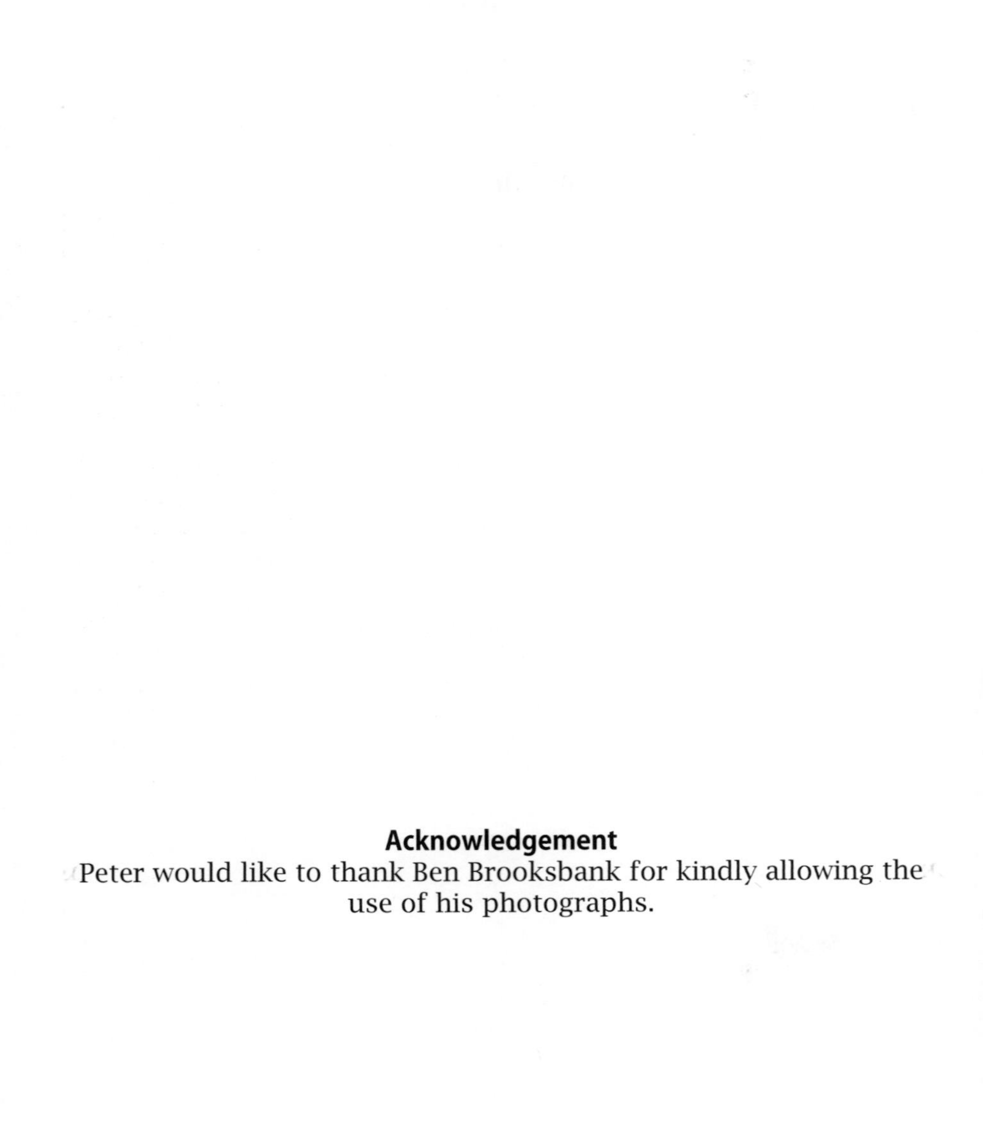

Acknowledgement

Peter would like to thank Ben Brooksbank for kindly allowing the use of his photographs.

Introduction

There are really two types of train station walks covered in this book. There are those from existing train stations that still have passengers bustling about them, and there are those from platforms that fell silent in the infamous closures of the 1960s. Whether you are wanting to reach your starting point via train or delve into the history of transport in the Peak District, this book has something for you - and it will take you to some startling scenery as you explore the 20 walks included.

The Hope Valley Line is still in use today and sees thousands of people every day using its trains, some to commute to Sheffield and Manchester, while others get off the slower train in the Peaks to go walking. There are certainly many beautiful places that this train line can take you to, and there are walks in this book heading out from Edale, Chinley, Hope, Hathersage, Grindleford and Bamford. Each one is different, but they all take in the best the national park has to offer while also giving you the chance to leave the car at home as you plan a day out in the Peak District.

Other railway stations in the Peak District were not so fortunate when the Beeching Axe was being wielded in the 1960s. Among them, Monsal Dale, Thorpe and Tissington were incredibly popular with ramblers at the time and many people used the trains to have a day out exploring the fantastic walking country. Today, sadly, you can't get out to these places using train services, but the closure of the lines also leaves us with a popular legacy in the walking routes that follow the once busy railway lines. The Tissington Trail, Monsal Trail and High Peak Trail have thousands of visitors each week making use of their ideal walking and cycling tracks, while at the same time gaining a sense of history by enjoying the features of the railway that have survived the closure. Walks from former stations such as Hassop, Parsley Hay or Bakewell will allow you to glimpse at disused stations, once-busy platforms, tunnels, viaducts, old signal houses and even lengthy tunnels constructed in Victorian times to help navigate the difficult terrain.

One thing all the train station walks have in common is that they enjoy fabulous routes into some breath-taking countryside. Gorges, woodland, moors, farmland, rivers, glacial valleys and some tremendous hills are all included in this series of 20 walks, linked together by the transport routes that, today and in the past, dissected the Peak District.

Peter Naldrett, 2013
www.peter-naldrett.co.uk
Twitter: @peternaldrett

Penistone Station on the Woodhead Line, 1954 *(photograph © Ben Brooksbank)*

Walk 1
Bakewell

A circular walk across fields and along a disused railway from the National Park's only town to a great country house.

The Monsal Trail

The majority of the route you can walk along today was opened up in 1981, though back then several of the tunnels remained closed for safety reasons and paths diverted visitors around them. Large black doors, locked and imposing, blocked off the tunnels, though you used to be able to go right up to them, peer into the dark through the tiny gap in the middle and feel the cold draught of wind blowing through. A new lease of life was breathed into the Monsal Trail in May 2011, when four tunnels were reopened, making it a through route once more. The ability to walk, bike or take your horse through Headstone Tunnel, Cressbrook Tunnel, Litton Tunnel and Chee Tor Tunnel made the Monsal Trail a national gem among walking routes and started to pull in larger numbers of ramblers.

The total length of the trail is 8.5 miles, from Coombs Road Viaduct near Bakewell to Blackwell Mill in Wyedale. As you can gauge from this book, there are plenty of points to access the trail. The best places to start your walks are the former train stations that now house car parks, including Bakewell, Hassop and Millers Dale. And, whichever of these walks you decide to begin with, there are both industrial and natural features that will add extra interest to the amazing scenery. Be it the atmospheric cotton mills at Cressbrook and Litton, the lime kilns along the route that took advantage of the new transport, the breath-taking viaducts, the wildlife reserves or the plethora of fossils in the limestone, this is a fascinating area to explore.

Despite the huge popularity of the line as a walking and biking trial, there are some who want to see the Monsal Trail reopen as a train line as part of an environmental drive to improve public transport. In 2004, a feasibility study was carried out by Derbyshire County Council and its partners to decide if reopening was a possibility. The £100 million cost to convert it back into a railway line was considered too much to get the project the green light in the foreseeable future.

Network Rail did not include the line when setting out plans for the region's rail up to 2019, though it was mentioned in the appendix as a route that some want to see developed once more. There is the glimmer of hope for rail enthusiasts that engines will once again head through these famous tunnels.

Bakewell Station

Standing half a mile outside the town centre, Bakewell's station buildings are grander than you may expect for a rural settlement. Featuring detailed coat of arms carvings, the extra effort was put into this station because it was the one used by the Duke of Rutland, based at nearby Haddon Hall. The railway line was allowed to pass through the Duke's land on its way to Bakewell, following detailed negotiations about using the estate and an agreement to create a tunnel that would keep trains hidden from sight. Opened on August 1st, 1862, it was immediately popular with tourists coming to the region and especially busy when the annual Bakewell Show was hosted. With the rise of the car and the fall of the Beeching Axe, Bakewell Station was closed in 1967 and is now the site of an industrial estate and the popular Monsal Trail.

Bakewell Pudding

Not to be confused with a Bakewell Tart, the Bakewell Pudding has its origins in the town and has now become synonymous with this part of Derbyshire. A sweet dish that is certainly not to everybody's taste, such a fabulously local product is definitely worth seeking out and sampling once your walk in the town is complete. There is more than one outlet in Bakewell which sells the distinctive pudding and more than one which holds a claim to the original recipe. The actual roots of the Bakewell Pudding is up for debate, but a common tale is that it was baked by mistake in 1820 at the pub now called The Rutland Arms. The story goes that the landlady at the time asked her cook to produce a jam tart and got the recipe confused, spreading a mixture of eggs and almonds on top of the jam rather than mixing it with the pastry. The result became popular at the pub and so was born a legendary dish that still has tourists flocking to the town today.

Route

From the pay and display car park at the train station, head beyond the station buildings to the Monsal Trail and turn right onto it,

Length	**6.3km / 3.9miles**
Allow	**1 hour 40 minutes**
Terrain	**Some steep sections and some of the paths could be muddy after rain**
Refreshments	**Although nothing lies directly on the route, it's possible to arrange your own diversion to Chatsworth from Edensor for the cafés and restaurants there. Closer to the route, when you leave the road and enter the wood on the way back to the station, look out for Ball Cross Farm, which has a tea room**
Getting there	**Bakewell is well signposted on the area's roads and can be found on the A6 between Rowsley and Ashford in the Water. Once in Bakewell, take the A619 across the bridge and immediately after this take the road off to the right. Follow this up the hill until you come to the old station, which is now the site of the Monsal Trail. Grid reference SK 222, 689**
Next stations	**When trains rattled along this route, passengers could be linked to Hassop to the north east and Rowsley to the south west**
Map	**OS Outdoor Leisure 24 White Peak Area**

heading under the bridge. You'll soon be able to see the town of Bakewell on the right. Just before reaching the second bridge on the trail, turn left and head up the bank, turning left at the top and going towards the golf course. As you go across the small section of the golf course, ring the bell to let the players know you are there and then enter Manners Wood at the other side.

Head across a stream in the wood, entering the Haddon Estate, and take the path soon after on the left that doubles back on itself. When you reach another stream, turn right and head up the hill, passing a

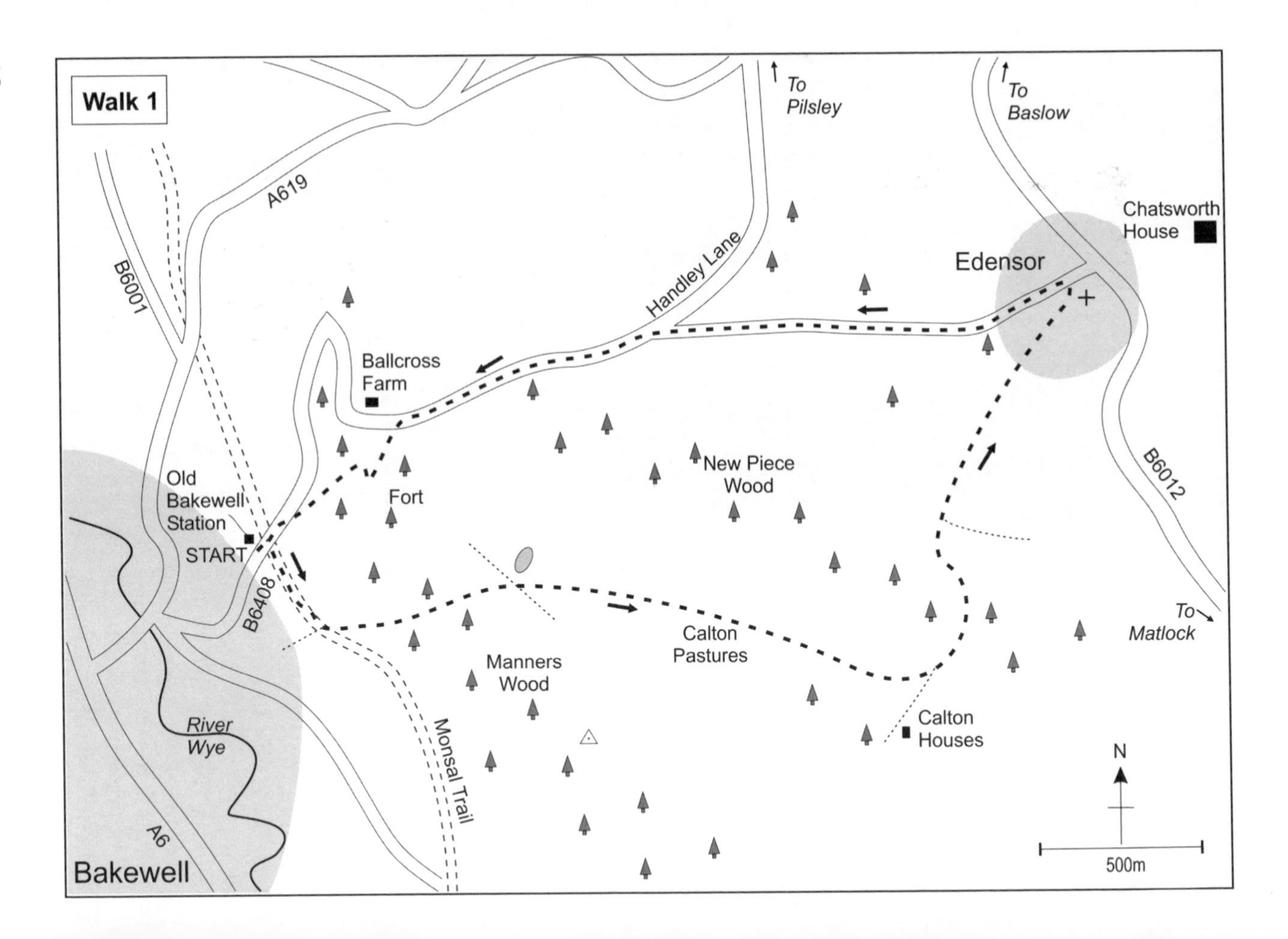
Walk 1
To Pilsley
To Baslow
A619
Handley Lane
Chatsworth House
Edensor
B6001
Ballcross Farm
New Piece Wood
Old Bakewell Station
START
Fort
B6408
B6012
To Matlock
Calton Pastures
Manners Wood
River Wye
Monsal Trail
Calton Houses
N
A6
Bakewell
500m

Bakewell Station in 1905 *(www.picturethepast.org.uk)*

ruined building and reaching a gate at the edge of the wood. You now come out onto Calton Pastures, a large area of farm land at the top of the hill, with the path you are taking bearing off to the right. Pass a small wood on the left, go through a gate and head past a small pond on your left. Follow the path which bears left towards Chatsworth and follow this through the middle of the field. Go over the stile and enter the next field, carrying on until you meet another path signed for Edensor and Chatsworth. Turn left onto this and enter New Piece Wood.

Heading out of the wood, you walk into the Chatsworth Estate and can clearly see the house. This is a deer park, so keep your eye out for them roaming around. Continue straight ahead on the path down the field, aiming for the church spire you can see in Edensor. When you reach the edge of the village, go through the gate and down the steps into the centre. At the bottom of the steps, turn left onto the track and continue straight ahead.

The track eventually comes to an end at a road known as Handley Lane and you should turn left onto this. Look out for Stanage Edge across to the right. When the road bends sharply to the right, you need to take the path straight on through the woods – though first you may like a diversion to Ball Cross Farm tea room a little down the road on the right.

The path winds a steady way down through the wood and then once more across the golf course. It brings you out at a road, where you should turn left. Crossing over the bridge, you can see the station on the right and from here make your way back to the starting point.

The descent to Edensor through the Chatsworth Estate

Walk 2
Hassop

A nice café and book shop occupy the building that used to be Hassop Station, making this a very pleasant starting point for a walk along the Monsal Trail and over fields towards Bakewell.

Hassop Station

Sited a couple of miles to the south of the village of Hassop, the station was opened on August 1st, 1862, as part of a line being built between Rowsley and Buxton. When the station first opened its doors, the line had only been built to Hassop and so it was a temporary terminus for nearly a year until the rest of the track was laid. Passengers could travel from here to Buxton and Derby and, although long distance services never stopped here, the local people could connect to them at other stations and it opened up a wealth of possibilities. The remote location proved crucial in the downfall of the station, though, because many hotels and businesses preferred to use Rowsley Station over Hassop and the number of people using the station started to decline at the turn of the 20th century. Sunday services were scrapped in 1921 and other trains were slowly withdrawn until there were none remaining by 1942. Hassop continued as a goods yard before closing entirely in 1964. Today, the resurgence of The Monsal Trail's popularity has led to a revival at Hassop. You'll see today that there is a thriving café, bookshop and cycle hire shop based in the building that once was a gateway for Victorian passengers.

Hassop

Although the station was given the name of Hassop, it is a decent walk from the village to the platform. Hassop, of course, has origins going way back beyond the invention of the railway. The village was mentioned in the Doomsday book as Hetesope and was the main home of the Faljambes before passing to the Plumpton family. At the end of the 15th century, Hassop was sold to the Eyre family, who were Catholic and experienced much persecution during the reign of Elizabeth I. It was the Eyre family who built the first Hassop Hall in the 17th century, and circumstances of the day saw them defending it against Parliamentarians in 1643 when the Kings army had a garrison here during the Civil War. When the

Down empty stock train passing the remains of Hassop Station
(photograph © Ben Brooksbank)

Parliamentarians led by Oliver Cromwell won the war, the hall was seized and Rowland Eyre had to pay the princely sum of £21,000 - then an absolutely fortune - to get it back. The house was updated several times through the years and passed from the Eyre family into the Leslie family in the 1850s after Mary Eyre died and left it to her widower, Charles Leslie. Hassop Hall was sold to the Stephenson family in 1919 until sold to be developed into a country hotel in 1975.

Now a luxury destination for weddings and romantic breaks, Hassop Hall pulls off the manorial image with gusto, flaming torches lighting the driveway when celebrations are taking place. Yet while many people are now employed in accommodation and catering at the hall, the real industrial driving force that helped build Hassop took place underground. The village started to grow and the population increased because of the lead mines that were developed here and went by such names as The Brightside and Harry Bruce. These mines, of which there were several, were operating until the middle of the 19th century, by which time Hassop was well established and about to be connected to the rest of the world via the steam train.

Creating the trail

Once a thriving railway line providing a lifeline for villages in this part of the Peak District, the axe finally came in 1968 when the then Labour Minister for Transport, Barbara Castle, decided to shut the line at the time when the industry was still reeling from the Beeching closures. The tracks were taken up and the line was unused for 12 years until the Peak District National Park took it over and created the 8.5 mile Monsal Trail route, which runs from the Coombs Road Viaduct to Topley Pike Junction at Wye Dale. Featured as one of Julia Bradbury's TV *Railway Walks*, The Monsal Trail has always been a popular route for walkers, bikers and horse riders. But that popularity has increased since the £3.78 million project was completed in 2011 that saw four extra tunnels opened to the public. Now a much more direct route, the tunnels also bring a sense of history to life and make a wander along the Monsal Trail an extremely valuable outing.

Length	5km/3.1 miles
Allow	1 hour 30 minutes
Terrain	Most of the walk is along well established bridleways and cycling paths, although some sections have a slight incline and the paths can get muddy after heavy rain
Refreshments	The start of the walk is the old Hassop Railway Station which has now been converted into a popular café serving drinks, snacks and meals (grid reference SK 217, 705)
Getting there	The site of the former Hassop Railway Station is easily accessible by road. The A6020 loops off the A6 at Ashford in the Water and it is at the junction of the A6020 and the B6001 where you'll find the starting point
Next stations	On this disused line, Hassop is the station inbetween Bakewell to the south east and the west-bound stop at Great Longstone
Map	OS Outdoor Leisure 24 White Peak Area

Route

From the old Hassop Station building, head for the Monsal Trail and turn right onto it, following the sign for Wye Dale. After a short time there is a bridleway that crosses the Monsal Trail and you should turn left onto it, going through a gate and heading up the short incline. At the top of the first hill, you go through a couple of gates and then pass through another soon after. Continue on along the path and pass through another gate at the top of the next hill, getting a good view of Bakewell on the way down the other side. After another couple of gates, you'll see a path off to the right signed for Great Longstone and you should take this as it cuts back on your route.

Head across the field and you'll come to a gate entering another field, where the path heads off to the right. Continue ahead, passing a farm building on the left. When you pass this and enter the next field, the path bears off to the left and heads towards a small wood. Climb over the stile and enter the wood, following the path as it winds through the trees until you pass through a gate and cross over a field.

The Monsal Trail cuts through the limestone region of the Peak District

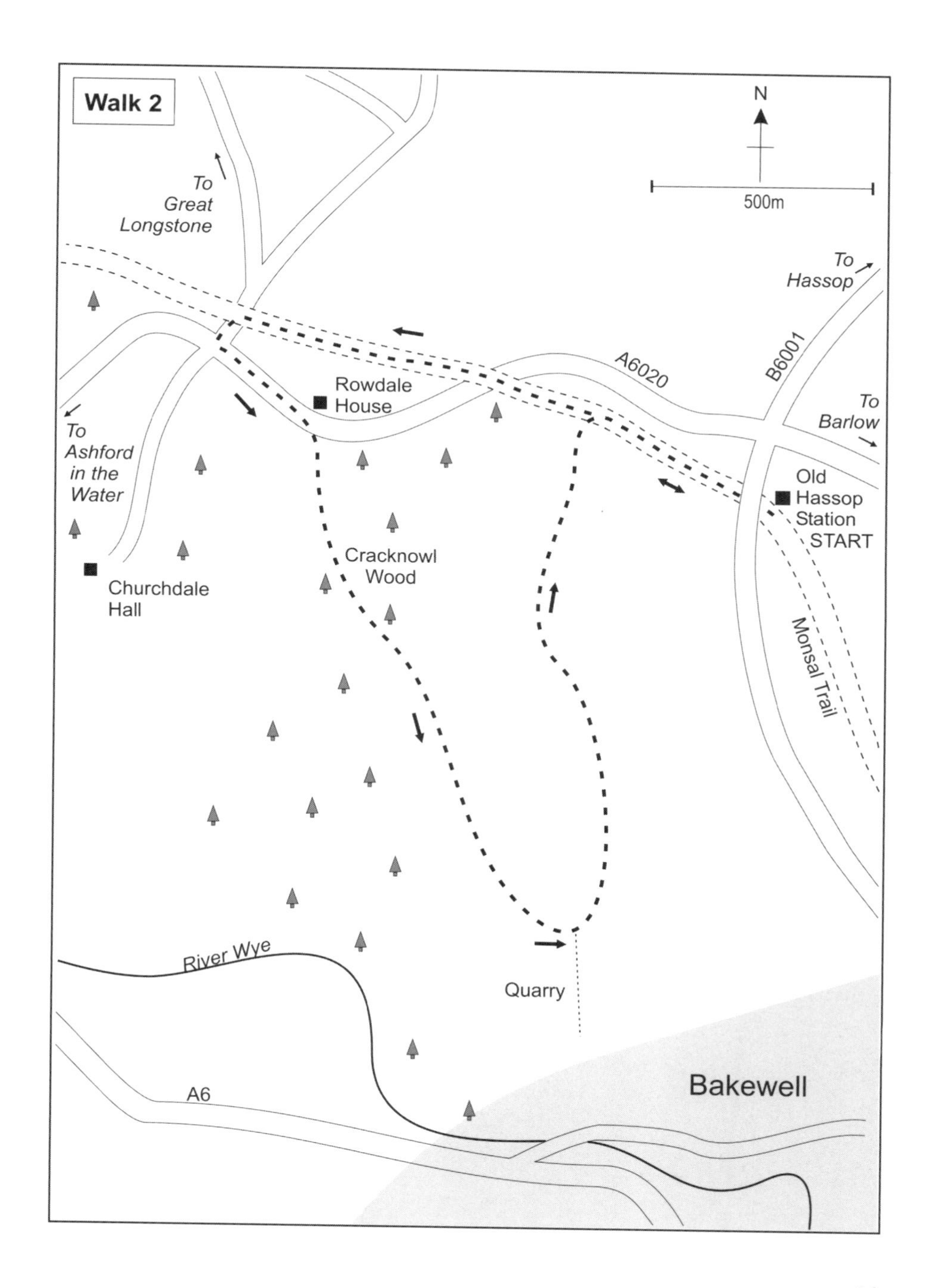
Walk 2
N
500m
To Great Longstone
To Hassop
B6001
A6020
To Barlow
Rowdale House
To Ashford in the Water
Old Hassop Station START
Cracknowl Wood
Churchdale Hall
Monsal Trail
River Wye
Quarry
A6
Bakewell

At the end of the field, you reach the A6020 road and you need to turn left onto it. Soon after, take the road off to the right signed for Great Longstone and Rowland. Under the bridge, take the road on the right for Hassop and Rowland, and immediately after enter the path signed back to the Monsal Trail. When you get onto the trail again, turn left and follow it until it takes you back to Hassop Station.

Walk 3
Monsal Dale

A round walk by Cressbrook Mill, this is a short stroll to enjoy the sights of the Wye Valley near Monsal Head, taking in a stretch of the Monsal Trail as you go.

Caption here

Monsal Dale Station

When you approach the site of the former Monsal Dale Station, you will still be able to see the remains of the platform where people could catch the train south to Bakewell. On the other side of the rails was a wooden platform that is no longer in existence, just like the original wooden station buildings that were brought here from Evesham Station in Worcestershire. Opened in 1866, the station was originally intended to be for goods heading to and from Cressbrook Mill, but passenger services were later added so surrounding villages could benefit from the line. The station is certainly in a quaint, rural and picturesque setting, but this was not enough to keep it open. Monsal Dale Station finally closed in 1960.

Headstone Viaduct

One of the most recognisable views in this part of Derbyshire is not a natural one, which is surprising for such a beautiful location. It's actually a constructed piece of engineering that was condemned as being an eyesore when it first made an appearance on the Monsal Dale skyline in 1863. Undoubtedly a masterpiece of engineering in the Victorian age, the Headstone Viaduct is often wrongly referred to as the Monsal Dale Viaduct, but the impression it leaves is great, irrespective of the name. It spans an area of 91 metres and was the cure for the planning headache handed to the railway companies in the form of hills, valleys and the steep gradients linking them.

Getting from one side of a hill to the other without skirting round the edge above a steep ravine is easy enough - you can just build a tunnel. But when you come out of that tunnel and are instantly greeted with a large, curving valley, you need to use extra measures to keep the railway line as flat as was possible. The result was the Headstone Viaduct, a marvellous bridge crossing Monsal Dale that greeted the eyes of passengers the moment they came out of the Headstone Tunnel. The bright, brilliant views of the limestone peaks were as big a contrast with the darkened tunnel as it was possible to imagine and the sight on emergence from the black became renowned.

But while the structure became listed in 1970 and is generally well photographed and liked, the Headstone Viaduct was the subject of derision when it was first used to carry trains through the Peak District. Leading social commentator John Ruskin was a severe critic of the viaduct and wrote: "The valley is gone, and the Gods with it; and now, every fool in Buxton can be in Bakewell in half an hour, and every fool in Bakewell at Buxton; which you think is a lucrative process of exchange - you Fools everywhere."

Cressbrook Mill

Famous factory pioneer Richard Arkwright was responsible for the first of the Cressbrook Mill buildings, later developed further by his son and Henry McConnel. Indeed, before the coming of the mill Cressbrook did not exist as a village at all; the surrounding houses were developed to house the workers there. The most significant expansion of the housing was taken under McConnel's reign, when the workforce objected to their current standard of accommodation. He decided to build a model village in the 1830s and this was extended in the decades that followed. In the 1960s the mill ceased to operate and has now been converted into apartments.

Length	2.9km/1.8 miles
Allow	1 hour
Terrain	Good footpaths throughout, including a section of the Monsal Trail. Some slopes to negotiate
Refreshments	Nothing directly on the route, but nearby Monsal Head has the Monsal Head pub serving meals. www.monsalhead.com Tel: 01629 640250
Getting there	The walk starts at a car park just to the east of Cressbrook at Upperdale (grid reference SK 176, 721). To reach it, head for the B6465 which runs between Bakewell and a junction with the A623. In the middle of this road you will reach Monsal Head. Turn off here for the pub and follow the local road down the hill towards Cressbrook. The car park will be on your left
Next stations	When goods were loaded on trains from the mill, they either went in the direction of Longstone to the south east or to Millers Dale to the north west
Map	OS Outdoor Leisure 24 White Peak Area

Route

From the car park at Upperdale, head towards the small hamlet and turn right, heading down towards a bridge. Cross over the bridge and walk up the track on the other side which takes you under a bridge. From here, make your way round the other side to the Monsal Trail and turn left onto it, following the signs for Wye Dale.

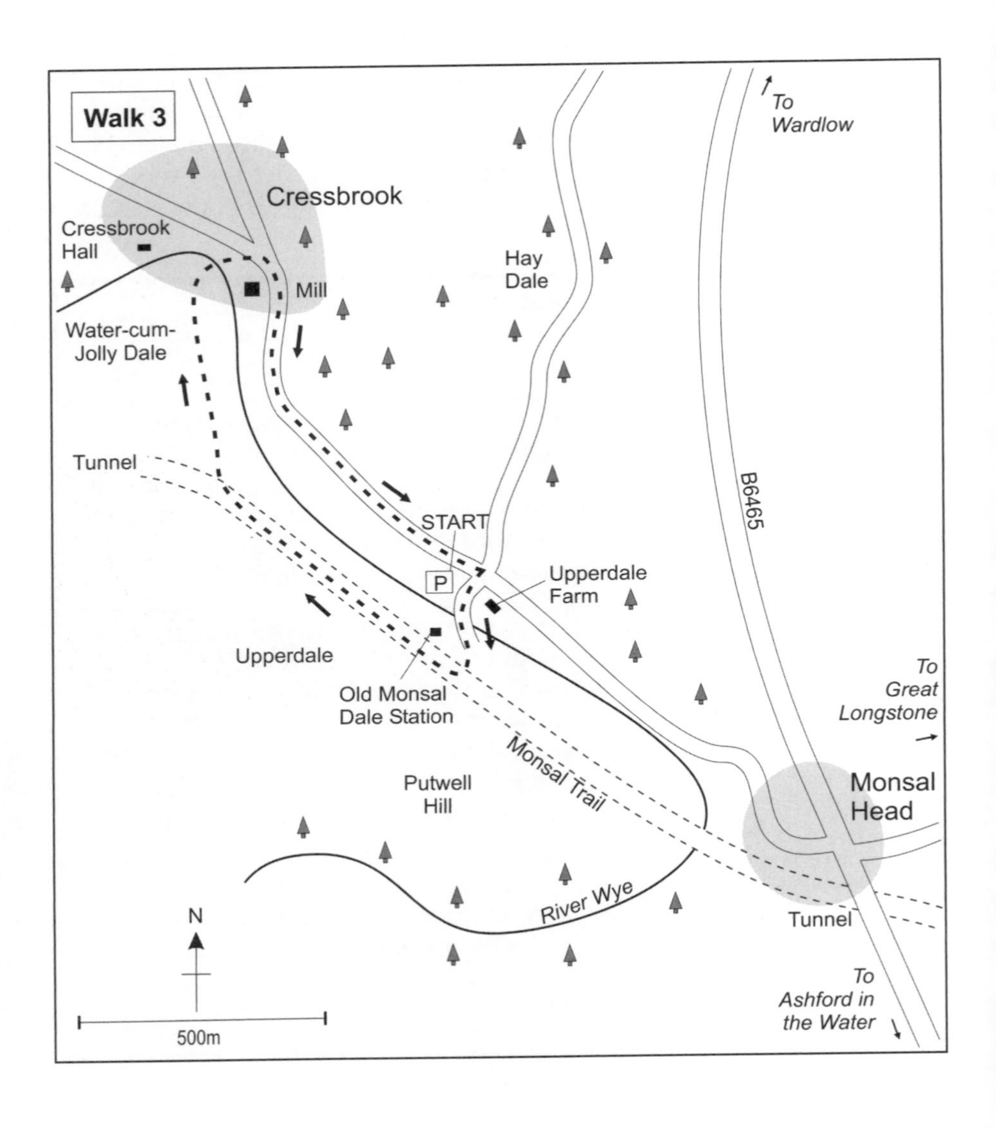

It's a simple enough walk along this section of the trail and you'll soon find yourself approaching the Cressbrook Tunnel, opened in 2011 to allow walkers and cyclists access. But this route doesn't go through the tunnel, instead following the path that the Monsal Trail used to be diverted along. So just before the tunnel, take the path off to the right

Cressbrook Mill from the Monsal Trail

with Cressbrook Mill in full view before you. This path, signed for Cressbrook, takes you down the hill and towards the river. Head over the bridge at the bottom and turn right towards the mill. The path takes you by the side of the old mill building, now converted into flats. When you reach the road, turn right onto it and continue until you get back to the car park.

Walk 4
Great Longstone for Ashford

From the grand surroundings off Thornbridge Hall, along the Monsal Trail, through historic railway tunnels and passing several pubs giving you the chance of a rest, this is an ideal short countryside walk.

The Headstone Viaduct, looking down from Monsal Head

Great Longstone for Ashford Station

When it first opened in 1863, the station was named simply Longstone. But in 1913, in an attempt to widen the appeal of the station and the railway in general, it was given the new name of Great Longstone for

Ashford, referring to nearby Ashford-in-the-Water. When you set off on this walk and arrive back, you'll be able to see several remnants from the days when trains called in here. The station platforms are still intact and you'll have to walk along one of them to get to the former track bed, now part of the Monsal Trail. The old station building is also still standing and now is a house that stands behind a new fence built along the other platform. Standing on the nearby railway bridge looking down on the scene from the road, you get a sense of what this site would have been like when carriages squeaked to a halt here.

Great Longstone

Mentioned in the Doomsday book as Longsdune and having a price of 30 shillings attached to it, Great Longstone is a nice place to visit after the walk and there are a couple of pubs to help rest aching feet. The church of St Giles is one of the key landmarks in the village, along with Longstone Hall which was rebuilt in the 18th century as the area prospered thanks to lead mining and shoe making. One of the pubs is named The Crispin Inn and offers a clue to the village's past, St Crispin being the patron saint of shoemakers. A limestone ridge lies to the north of the village and is a well known beauty spot, but one which has a controversial history. Quarrying has long been an industry associated with Longstone Ridge, though there has been strong local pressure and legal battles to bring this to an end.

Thornbridge Hall

The old station building you can still see at the former Great Longstone for Ashford station, was given its grand design to keep it in keeping with nearby Thornbridge Hall. An intriguing building that has had numerous industrious owners over the years, the origins of Thornbridge Hall actually date back to the 12th century. More complete records of its history begin when textile dealer John Morewood bought the hall in 1790 for £10,000, while new owner Frederick Craven had it rebuilt in 1859 and Sheffield businessman George Marples extended it to pretty much its current form in 1896. The big-business names continued to influence Thornbridge Hall when Sheffield entrepreneur, Charles Boot, owned the house from 1929 and changed the feel of the place considerably by bringing in many fountains, statues and facades from Clumber Park when a fire caused damage there in 1938. From 1945 Sheffield City Council owned the hall and used it as a teacher training college. It is now privately owned and closed to the public, but available to hire for weddings and events. www.thornbridgehall.co.uk

Length	3.1km/1.9 miles
Allow	1 hour 20 minutes
Terrain	There is a short, sharp climb up to the pub and café at Monsal Head when you emerge from the Headstone Tunnel. Other parts of the route are gentle
Refreshments	A range of places are passed directly on the route. The Monsal Head pub serves a range of meals (01629 640815 www.monsalhead.com), while lighter meals are available at the tea rooms next door (01629 640346 www.hobbsmonsalhead.co.uk). When you walk through Little Longstone, the Packhorse Inn welcomes walkers for food and drink (01629 640471 www.packhorselongstone.co.uk)
Getting there	The start of the walk is on Longstone Lane, at the old railway bridge that crosses the Monsal Trail next to where Great Longstone for Ashford Station once stood – grid reference SK 198, 711. To reach Longstone Lane, head for one of the two villages providing good access, either Great Longstone or Ashford-in-the-Water. From Great Longstone, follow the sign for Thornbridge Hall from the middle of the village and from Ashford take the B6465 towards Monsal Head before turning right along Longstone Lane. There is road side parking either side of the railway bridge near Thornbridge Hall
Next stations	For nearly 100 years between 1863 and 1962, Great Longstone for Ashford was the station linking Hassop and Monsal Dale
Map	OS Outdoor Leisure 24 White Peak Area

Route

Once you're at the railway bridge over the Monsal Trail, head down the sloping path that takes you onto to one of the old platforms that made up this station. You'll be able to see the old station house on the left. Carry on along to the end of the platform before joining the Monsal Trail and continuing straight ahead. This is a simple path to follow and fields will soon open up on the left and right to reveal the surrounding countryside. You'll notice that the track here is built up on an embankment to keep the track level; soon after the route enters a railway cutting that had to be blasted out for exactly the same reason. This cutting, just before the Headstone Tunnel, was created in 1860 as the line was being created.

You can't fail to be impressed by the imposing entrance of the Headstone Tunnel as you approach it. Simply disappearing into the hillside, this lengthy 490 metre long tunnel was an essential piece of engineering to create the new railway and take those coming from Bakewell into Monsal Dale. Closed since the 1960s, you can now enter these underground passages thanks to a multi-million pound restoration project and this walk continues through the Headstone Tunnel.

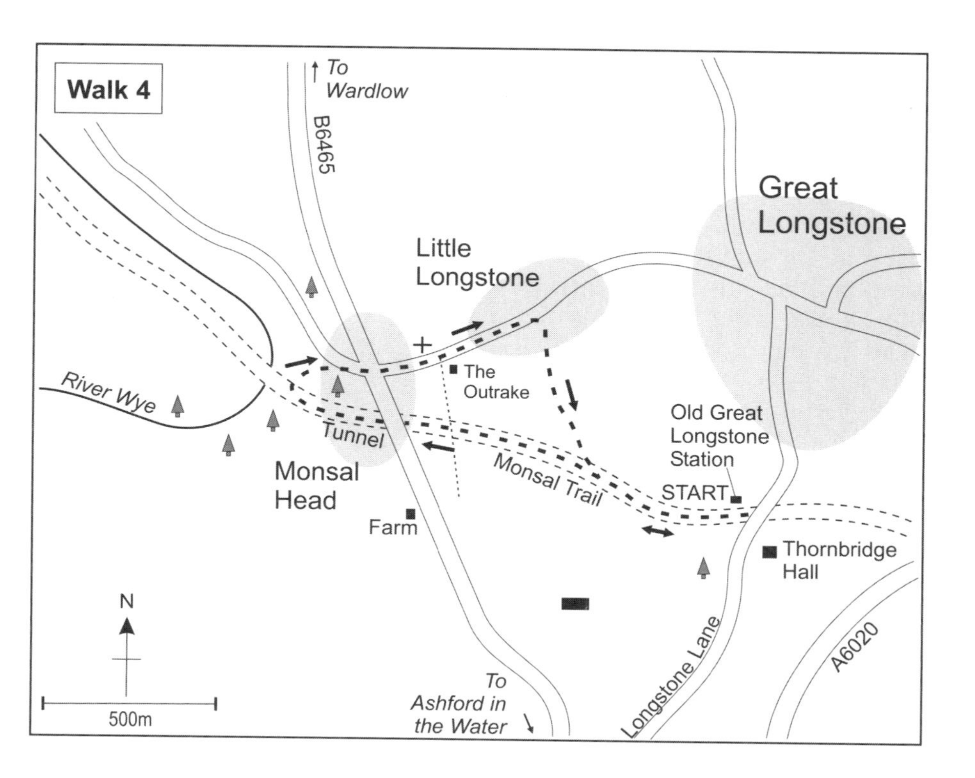

Coming out at the other end of the tunnel delivers you to one of Derbyshire's most magnificent places: Monsal Dale. Although it's a pleasure to explore the Headstone Viaduct just ahead of the tunnel entrance, the real vantage point here is at the top of the hill and that is why, just after the tunnel, the route for this walk takes the path off to the right. Keep climbing the hill, following signs to Monsal Head. Eventually you will come out at the pub and café at the top, and here is the point to glance down on the viaduct and imagine steam trains puffing along the valley.

Head beyond the pub to the road. Cross over and take the road turning off the B6465 towards Great Longstone. Continue into the village of Little Longstone, passing the pub on your left. As the road dips a little, look out for a footpath on your right signed for the Monsal Trail. Take this and head straight across the field. Climb a stile into the next field and bear left alongside the railway embankment. When you join the Monsal Trail, turn left and head back to Great Longstone, turning up the path when you reach the station's bridge.

The entrance to the newly restored Headstone Tunnel

The Monsal Trail runs from Bakewell to Wye Dale, passing Monsal Head on the way

Walk 5
Millers Dale

This is a route which will take you through two less-explored gems of the Peak District, Peter Dale and Monk's Dale. With two sections of the walk joining the Limestone Way, it's a tricky one to beat!

Millers Dale

When you wander through the beautiful and remote countryside which surrounds Millers Dale, it's hard to imagine this tiny settlement housing one of the busiest stations on the Midland Line. The transformation of this unsuspecting neighbourhood where the River Wye winds through the hills of the Derbyshire Dales came in 1863 when the station opened and formed part of the extended line from Rowsley to Buxton. The reason why it became one of the most significant rural stations is because it formed a junction where passengers from Buxton could jump on or get down from

Millers Dale station goods train in 1957 *(photograph © Ben Brooksbank)*

services for Manchester and London. Such was the demand for services from here that in 1905 a second viaduct was added, along with two extra tracks and a third platform. Despite Millers Dale being a very popular junction, changing trains here did involve a wait that was lengthy at times and earned it the nickname Patience Station. Like many railway stations, the name has been changed over the years. At first this one was going to be called Blackwell Mill before Millers Dale was decided upon in 1863. By 1889, though, the name was revised to Millers Dale for Tideswell and this name stuck until 1965 when Millers Dale once again came into favour. Two years later, the station was closed. Memories of it live on, though, in the 1964 railway homage *Slow Train*, by Flanders and Swann, that immortalised Millers Dale along with other stations that were to close in the 60s.

Limestone Way

Cutting through the Derbyshire Dales, giving a wonderful cross section of rural life, the Limestone Way is a well used long distance footpath covering some 46 miles. Starting in Castleton, Derbyshire, and winding a steady way down to Rocester in Staffordshire, this is an intimate way to

The Limestone Way is a great route to see some wonderful rock features

get to know the nooks and crannies of the White Peak, the name handed to this part of the world because of the light coloured limestone. There are some big tourist attractions and lovely places to stay on the route, making the Limestone Way a great route to sample the joys of the Peaks over a few strenuous days. After Castleton, you've got Millers Dale, Flagg, Monyash, Youlgreave, Matlock, Tissington and Thorpe to look forward to.

Tideswell

Just to the north of Millers Dale, the village of Tideswell is home to nearly 2,000 people and holds the claim of being the second biggest settlement of the national park, after Bakewell. This is the station that people from Tideswell will have used, explaining why the station was at one time called Millers Dale for Tideswell. A pleasant village to visit at any time of the year, it is at its most colourful during Wakes Week – packed with festivities and the traditional well dressing. During this period you can experience a torchlight parade and the retelling of a local tale about a farmer whose cow got its head stuck in a gate... and so cut off its head to get it out!

Length	9.2km/5.7miles
Allow	3 hours
Terrain	This is a challenging route. There is a steep climb from the valley bottom to the Limestone Way at the beginning of the walk. The return through Millers Dale is very uneven, with limestone rocks to stride over and trees to duck under
Refreshments	There is often an ice cream van to be found at Millers Dale Station, while a tea room is also available in the house just above the station
Getting there	Millers Dale is sandwiched between the A6 near Buxton and the A623 near Chapel-en-le-Frith. The B6049 links these two roads and passes through Tideswell and Millers Dale. Once you're at Millers Dale, take the local road signed for the Monsal Trail and climb up to find to the car park on the left. Grid reference SK 138, 732

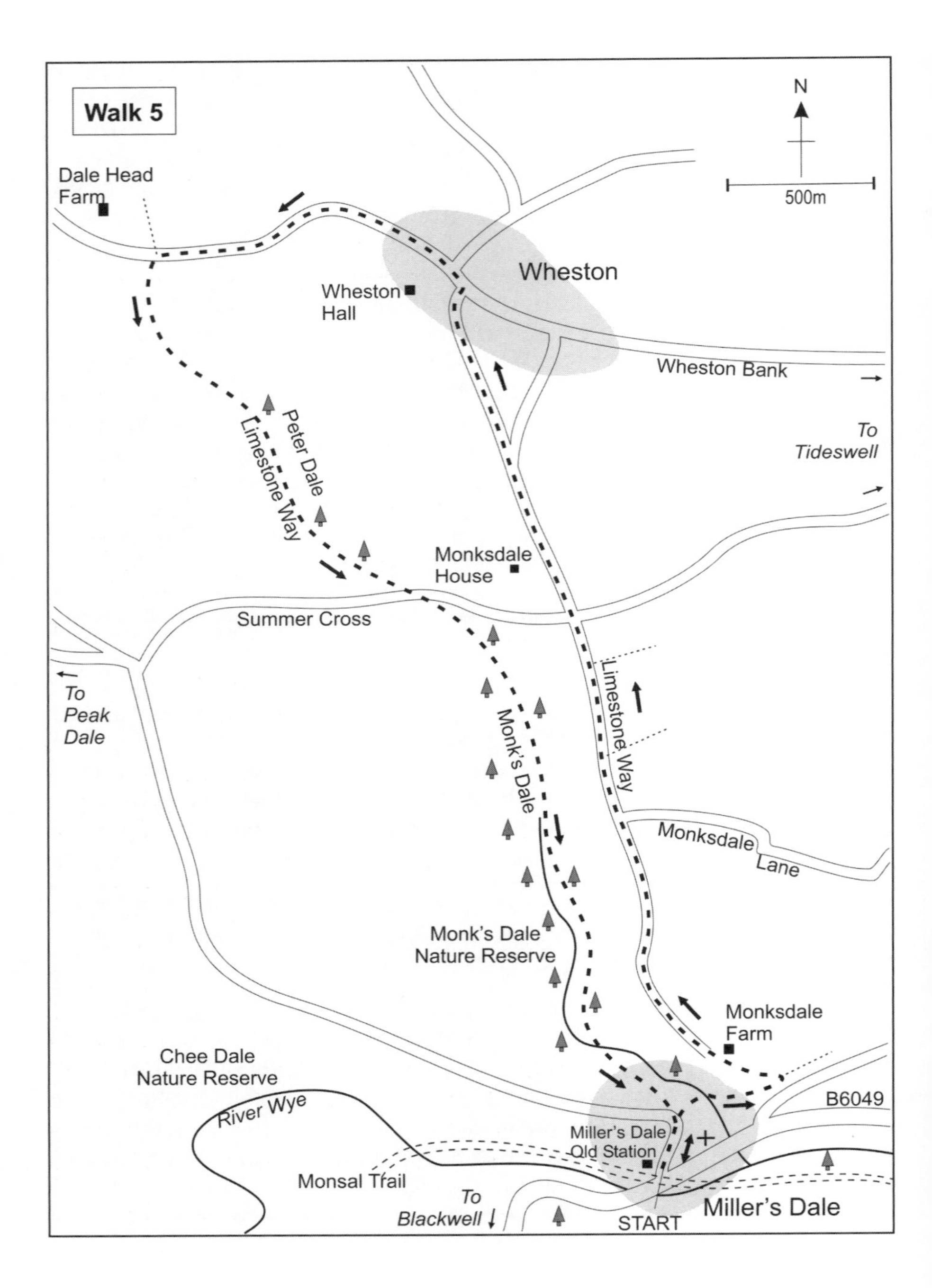

Walk 5
N
500m
Dale Head Farm
Wheston
Wheston Hall
Wheston Bank
To Tideswell
Peter Dale
Limestone Way
Monksdale House
Summer Cross
To Peak Dale
Monk's Dale
Limestone Way
Monksdale Lane
Monk's Dale Nature Reserve
Monksdale Farm
Chee Dale Nature Reserve
River Wye
B6049
Miller's Dale Old Station
Monsal Trail
To Blackwell
START
Miller's Dale

Next stations	Heading towards Bakewell, the next station would have been Monsal Dale. For those coming from Bakewell, trains headed for Blackwell Mill, unless they were on the New Mills Lane which called in at Peak Forest next
Map	OS Outdoor Leisure 24 White Peak Area

Route

Leave the car park and head towards the road, turning left onto it and climbing a short distance up the hill. When you reach the bend in the road, take the path off to the right. Go through a gate and into a field, following the path down the hill, from where you can see the two viaducts of the former railway. At the bottom of the field, a church comes into view and you make your way through a gate and down a set of stairs towards it. When you reach the main road, turn left and stick to the pavement until you cross the river – then take the track that heads up to the left. You will soon see a footpath signed off to the left for the Limestone Way and you need to take this.

Climbing the hill, stick to the Limestone Way as it goes through a gate and approaches Monksdale Farm, where you follow it to the left through a couple of gates. From here, it's a very easy and obvious path to follow as the Limestone Way climbs up over farmland and gives a great view of surrounding dales. Just keep an eye out for which way to go when you reach the gate at SK 138, 744 because the route takes a sharp left here. You'll then find yourself approaching a house where a road crosses the track you are on. Cross over here and continue ahead on the country road that doubles up as the Pennine Bridleway.

Take the track that forks off to the left when the road bends to the right and walk into the farming community of Wheston. When you reach the road, turn left and continue ahead as it bends to the left and then begins a steep descent. This is the point where the walk takes a stunning change in scenery as it ambles down into some classic Derbyshire Dales landscapes. When you reach the dip in the road, take the path to the left and enter Peter Dale across a field. Impressive limestone peaks on either side are an inspiring sight here in a wonderful dale that merits more visitors than it gets. At the end of the dale, cross the road and take the path opposite into Monk's Dale.

Looking down to St Anne's Church, Millers Dale

Although the route into Monk's Dale seems fairly ordinary at first, you are soon in for another scenery change as the atmosphere - and quality of the path - gets transformed. The surface now becomes extremely uneven and you have to keep your eyes open for limestone rocks and tree roots; but at the same time, keep your peepers peeled for a wide variety of birdlife, as well as some magnificent mosses and fine ferns that give this sheltered valley the air of a rainforest gulley. Before long, a stream can be made out on the right and you can literally see it get bigger and more substantial as the walk progresses. Further down, you cross this stream via a bridge and, on the other side, take a path that heads off to the left. This climbs up steadily and will bring you out to the field you crossed at the start of the walk. Turn right when you reach it and the path will bring you out to the road, where a short distance down the road to your left will bring you back to Millers Dale station on the right.

Walk 6
Rowsley

Through woodland and over moors from Rowsley, this lengthy walk starts off as a stroll by the River Derwent before climbing to Calton Houses and winding a tree-lined route back down to the A6.

The Manchester, Buxton, Matlock and Midland Junction Railway

It's a bit of a mouthful to say, but that's the official name that was given to this former track that linked Rowsley to Matlock and Buxton, and beyond to Manchester and London. To the west, much of the route is still preserved as part of the Monsal Trail, though around Rowsley it's fallen victim to main roads and shopping parks. There are groups who are campaigning to get the Monsal Trail extended this far, though the cost involved make it unlikely to happen. Initially this line was planned to link up with the east of England, but changes of plan led it to being part of Midland Railway's main line between London and Manchester.

The construction did not get off to a great start, though. The line reached Rowsley in 1849, but went no further due to a lack of money. Despite thousands of tourists using the station to access the Chatsworth Estate, it was not until 1860 that permission was granted for a line to run across the Pennines from Rowsley to Buxton. But Buxton stands at over 1,000 feet above sea level and the company had never constructed a line through such tricky terrain. There were valleys to bridge and hills to tunnel under. In 1863, Rowsley became a through route for over 100 years. The end for the entire line between Matlock and Buxton came in 1968 and most of the track was taken up. Some of the route remains inaccessible, but the Monsal Trail keeps the memory alive to the west of the Coombs Road Viaduct near Bakewell. But some of the line does live on; Heritage Rail organisation Peak Rail now operates on the line between Rowsley South and Matlock and has plans to extend towards Bakewell when funding allows. There are campaigners that would even like to see trains run along the full length of the line again.

Rowsley Station

Right from the outset, Rowsley was a popular station. From its opening in June 1849 there were some 60,000 people a year who got off at Rowsley

An ancient tree lines the route near Calton Lees

to explore the nearby grandeur of Chatsworth House. Indeed, in 1867 when the station was moved and the track realigned to provide a through route to Manchester, the station was renamed Rowsley for Chatsworth. The new station was built to be fit for the lords and ladies visiting the Duke of Devonshire at Chatsworth. In 1891 there was a subway added to connect the two platforms, something which was not very common at the time. As well as providing access to the express trains bound for both Manchester and London, Rowsley was also a very important hub for goods trains. In the late 19th and early 20th centuries, a large amount of limestone left the Derbyshire Dales region on trains heading south and the trade books were balanced by the importing of coal from pits in Derbyshire and Nottinghamshire. From 1933 when Express Dairies constructed a creamery close to the station, Rowsley also became an important distribution centre for milk. Every day, milk wagons would leave Rowsley bound for Derby and London. The demise of certain railway lines because of the rise of the car is well documented, and for Rowsley the end came in 1967 – two years after the station was renamed Rowsley and Chatsworth was dropped from the title. Today the original station can still be seen in the centre of the Peak Village shopping centre. The second site of the station, after the 1867 rebuilding, was next to Old Station Avenue where the walk begins. None of these buildings remain.

Length	**8.2km/5.1miles**
Allow	**2 hours 30 minutes**
Terrain	**There are steep sections to the walk, always on good paths. Some roadside walking is needed, and there is a crossing at a busy road**
Refreshments	**Close to the start and end of the walk, you will pass The Peacock, an award winning pub and restaurant serving a variety of food and drink. www.thepeacockatrowsley.com Tel: 01629 733518**
Getting there	**The car park which is both the site of the former station and the start of this walk can be found at grid reference SK 258, 658. Heading from Bakewell on the A6, drive into Rowsley and you'll see the car park on the right just before the junction with the B6012. If you are going into Rowsley on the A6 from Matlock, you'll see the car park on the left just after the left hand bend and the turning for Beeley**
Next stations	**The next station for Manchester-bound trains would have been Bakewell, while to the south Rowsley South Station is still in use as part of the Peak Rail heritage line**
Map	**OS Outdoor Leisure 24 White Peak Area**

Route

From the free car park at Old Station Avenue, head for the A6 and turn left. Just before you get to the river, opposite the Grouse pub, you can see the embankments on the left and right where the trains used to cross at this point. Use the crossing to reach the other side of the A6 and turn

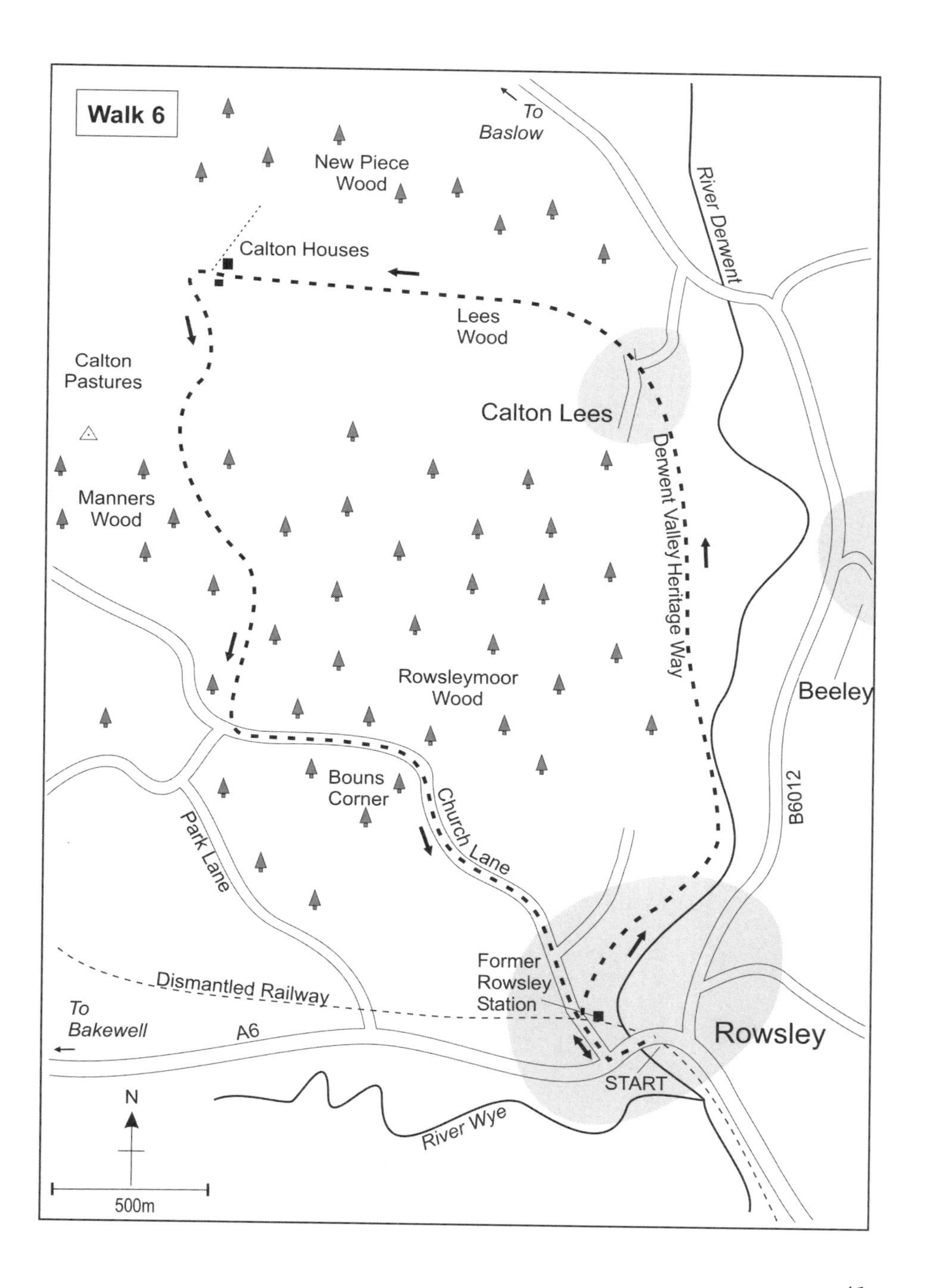
Walk 6
To Baslow
New Piece Wood
River Derwent
Calton Houses
Lees Wood
Calton Pastures
Calton Lees
Derwent Valley Heritage Way
Manners Wood
Rowsleymoor Wood
Beeley
Bouns Corner
Church Lane
Park Lane
B6012
Former Rowsley Station
Dismantled Railway
To Bakewell
A6
Rowsley
START
River Wye
N
500m

left onto it, before taking the road off to the right signed for the Post Office and the church. Soon after heading up this road, turn right on the path for Chatsworth and Calton Lees. This track takes you under the former railway bridge and you need to continue straight ahead with the river on your right.

The route continues and heads into a field, where there is often a chance to see varied wildlife, including Canada geese and pheasants. At the end of the field, climb over the stile and continue on the path, which actually forms the route of the Derwent Valley Heritage Way. Head over another stile and follow the path as it bends to the left with a hill off to the left showing a forest of pine trees. Go through a gap in the wall and stick the path straight ahead through the field, heading over the ladder and making your way towards Calton Lees. Turn right onto the road and follow it down the hill, turning left and taking the bridleway when you reach the T-junction at the bottom.

With fields on your right and a stream on your left, carry on up this well used track for just over 1km and you see Calton Houses ahead of

A young hiker makes his way over Calton Pastures

you on the right. When you are close to the houses, the path zig-zags up and goes through the middle of the small settlement. At the end of the track, go through a gate and take the path off to the left. The path soon bends around the left, going on the outside of a wood. Climb over a stile and take the path on the other side as it bends to the right and leaves the wood behind. You now have a fairly steep climb up the hill, with rolling countryside appearing on either side.

At the top of the path, climb over the ladder and enter the wood. This is a simple to follow path through the woods, taking you by some overhead power cables. Eventually you end up with a wall on the left and soon come to a junction of paths at the Haddon Estate, where you turn left onto the bridleway. At the next junction of paths (grid reference SK 244, 669), turn left onto the bridleway and head for Bouns Corner. Keep following the bridleway as it meanders through the woods and soon brings you to a gate; head down the track here, with a wall hemming you in on each side. The track eventually turns into a road, which in turn brings you out at the A6. Turn left onto it and cross over. Continue to head up the road and look out for Old Station Avenue on the right, which is the site of your car park.

Walk 7
Grindleford

A tea rooms gives you a feel of railway life of yesteryear, while the walk itself takes you up Padley Gorge by Burbage Brook and onto the National Trust's Longshaw Estate, through simply beautiful scenery.

Grindleford Station

Over 53,000 people use Grindleford Railway Station every year, many of them getting off here to explore the wonderful countryside nearby. Opened in 1894, the village of Grindleford lends its name to this stop, even though it lies a mile away and the nearest settlement is actually Nether Padley. The station buildings are still there and now house a great little café, the rooms of which are worth exploring for an historical

Grindleford Station, still in use on the Hope Valley

glimpse into the past. Trains on this line today rattle along the Hope Valley Line on the Northern Rail service between Sheffield and Manchester. There's also a limited service at Grindleford for the East Midlands trains running between Liverpool and Norwich.

Totley Tunnel

At the time it was built in 1893, the 3.5 mile long Totley Tunnel was the longest mainline railway tunnel in the country. Although that title now goes to the High Speed 1 link in East London, Totley Tunnel remains the longest tunnel that is not electrified. With the precise length of the tunnel displayed at the entrance (it's some 6,230 yards long), it took five years for workers to get this enduring piece of Victorian engineering finished. Numerous problems were encountered along the way, such as seeping water from the moors and the Duke of Rutland limiting the number of air shafts on his land while also stopping work during the grouse shooting season. Damp working conditions led to outbreaks of typhoid, diphtheria and scarlet fever among the workforce with living conditions contributing to this. Up to 30 people could be living in one of the few nearby houses with limited washing facilities, and some men even had to take turns at sleeping in the same bed.

Grindleford

Surrounded by National Trust land and hemmed in between Froggat Edge and Sir William Hill, Grindleford is dissected by the River Derwent and has Padley Gorge flowing to the north of it. Grindleford, then, is not only beautiful but also benefits from significant natural features and it was these that lay behind the village's initial development. With farming communities in the surrounding countryside, Grindleford was attractive because it was relatively sheltered and it was also a good point to cross the river - hence the name. An increasing number of people started to settle here, though at the start of the 19th century is was still a small, remote place with little more than 30 homes.

But the really significant event in the history of Grindleford was the coming of the railway into Hope Valley. When the line was built between Dore and Chinley, people from Sheffield and Manchester had the opportunity to explore the Peak District far more easily and, once they saw it, many decided to live here. The population rose steadily, as did the number of visitors. Soon Grindleford had shops, a pub, a church and, in 1876, a primary school where the local children are still taught today. The line, of course, survives and people still arrive here by train, many taking time to explore the intriguing station buildings that now house a café.

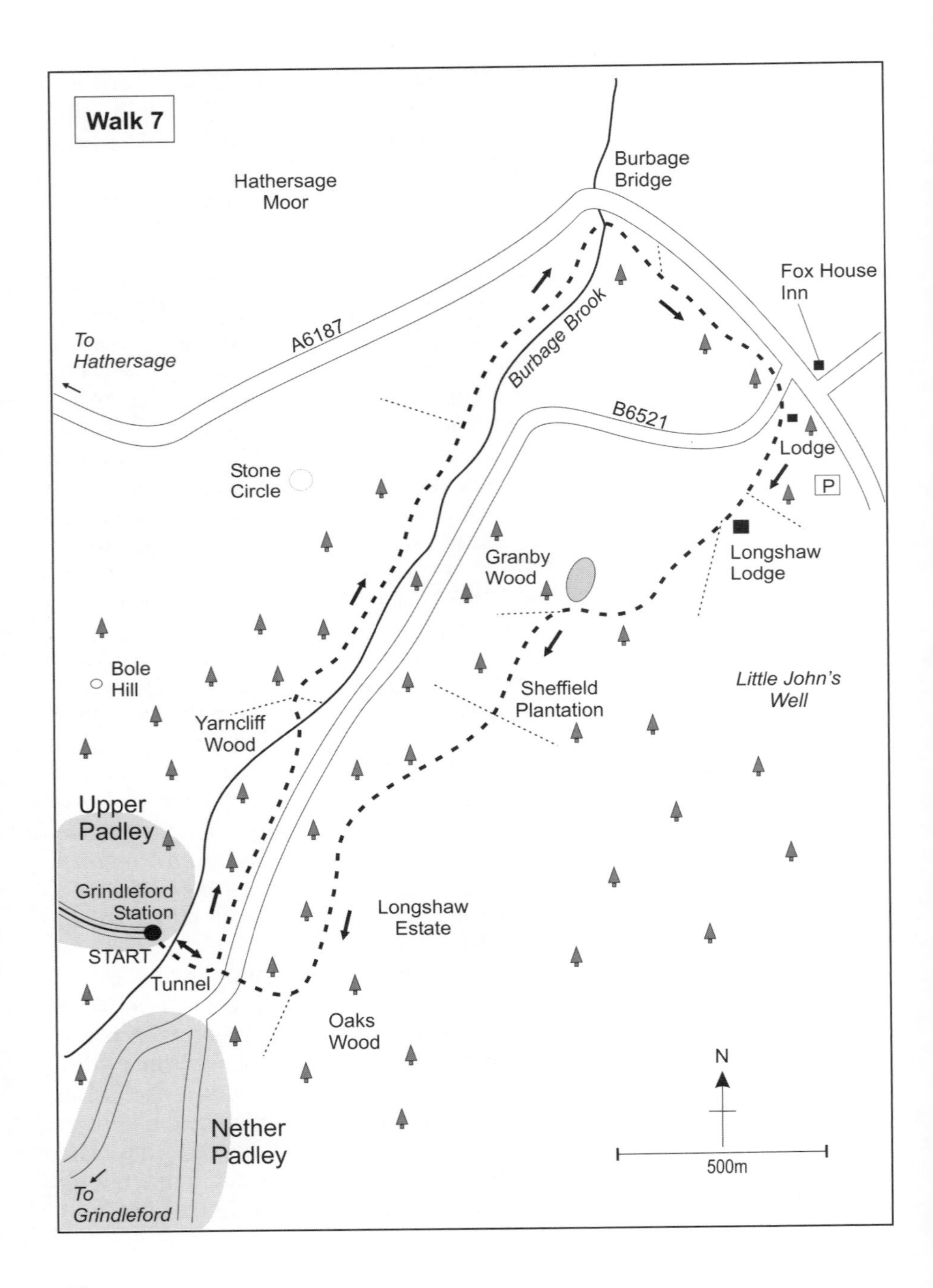
Walk 7
Hathersage Moor
Burbage Bridge
Fox House Inn
To Hathersage
A6187
Burbage Brook
B6521
Lodge
P
Stone Circle
Granby Wood
Longshaw Lodge
Bole Hill
Sheffield Plantation
Little John's Well
Yarncliff Wood
Upper Padley
Grindleford Station
START
Tunnel
Longshaw Estate
Oaks Wood
Nether Padley
To Grindleford
N
500m

Length	6.8km/4.2miles
Allow	2 hours 30 minutes
Terrain	Some of the path along Padley Gorge is rocky and there is a steep descent at the end of the route back to the railway station
Refreshments	The walk passes the café at Grindleford Station (SK 251, 787) as well as the National Trust café at the Longshaw Estate (SK 264, 798)
Getting there	Grindleford Railway Station is to be found north of Nether Padley on the B6521, south of Hathersage and north of Baslow. There is free parking on the lane down to the station. Grid reference SK 249, 788. Train journey times from Manchester are 59 minutes and from Sheffield 15 minutes
Next stations	Hathersage to the north west. Dore and Totley heading north east
Map	OS Outdoor Leisure 01 Dark Peak Area and Outdoor Leisure 24 White Peak Area

Route

The starting point for the walk is the entrance to Grindleford Railway Station, where the bridge crosses over the line and you get a close-up view of the lengthy Totley Tunnel. The former station building is now home to a café and it's on the right hand side of this that there is a path going up into the woods. Take this and climb the stairs, coming out at the B6521, where you need to turn left. Carry on along the pavement, passing the bus stop and then heading on the path into National Trust land signed as being the start of Padley Gorge.

The path takes you into Yarncliff Wood. Keep to the right when there is a fork in the route, continuing along the top side of the woods. Eventually you see Burbage Brook down to your left in Padley Gorge and soon after this there is a path that heads down the hill towards it. There are several places to cross the brook. Find a safe place to do so and make your way up the bank at the other side, joining the path and heading right along it.

The Longshaw Estate is a popular National Trust destination in the Peak District

Keeping the river on your right, continue along the path and eventually you need to head through a gate taking you into Access Land. The route becomes rockier here and the landscape really opens up, allowing views of Higger Tor and Carl Wark on the left. Stick to the path on the left hand side of the river, passing two footbridges as you press on. Just before the path reaches the main A6187 road, you need to cross over Burbage Brook on a footbridge at grid reference SK 260, 805. Continue along the path and enter the woods.

Soon after, look out for a path on the right and follow this as it climbs into the woods. This path brings you out at the B6521. Cross the road and head slightly to the right, where you will see the entrance to the Longshaw Estate – this is your next path and it will soon bring you out at the National Trust café on the left. From here, follow the sign for 'Estate Walks' and once you go through a gate take the path on the right. Going through a second gate, you can see a pond on the right and the path bends round to reach this.

At the pond, take the path off to the left signed for Yarncliff. You need to branch off to the right a couple of times on this path, following it down to a gate at grid reference SK 255, 790 where you enter Yarncliff Wood. Continue on this path, high above the road on the right. You can see the end approaching when you can make out the train tracks in the distance and although it doesn't appear this path will take you there at first, it does bend to the right and descend sharply down to the road. Cross the road and head down the path at the other side to come out once again at Grindleford Station.

Walk 8
Hathersage

Pick up the Derwent Valley Heritage Way and enjoy a wander through woods that stick close to the train route between Hathersage and Grindleford.

Hathersage station

Unlike many villages in the Peak District with railway stations, Hathersage's stopping point for trains is fairly close to the centre of the village. Just a short walk past a few houses from the central street in picturesque Hathersage, the station is within easy reach, has bus links and good parking spaces. Built in 1894, the original station

The railway at Hathersage is still well used by hikers and commuters

building was made of timber and eventually replaced with the more sturdy ones that remain today. The first reaction to the station in late Victorian times was not great and there was opposition to the train line being built close to the village. Hathersage, you see, had experience of a steam traction engine a few years before the station was officially opened, with residents seeing it churn up the roads as it pulled heavy carts and was involved in a fatal accident. Thankfully, today the railway is more popular and nearly 49,000 people make journeys from here every year.

Hathersage

There is plenty to entice visitors to stop off at Hathersage and so if you want to extend your stay after the walk you'll find it to be one of the busier of the Peak District villages. Aside from the usual collection of shops and cafés, many tourists will head for the church that has origins dating back to the late 14th century. There's history of local and national significance to be found here at St Micheal's, starting with a stained glass window removed from Derwent Chapel before it was submerged under Ladybower Reservoir. There is also a grave in the churchyard said to belong to Little John of Robin Hood fame. Fans of cult horror films may also recognise the church from *Living Dead at Manchester Morgue*, which had scenes filmed here in 1974.

Charlotte Bronte stayed in the village when penning *Jane Eyre* and the novel is thought to be full of local influence; Thornfield Hall in the novel is widely considered to be North Lees Hall, for example. Of course, many of the visitors these days who make their way to Hathersage do so to put on walking boots and take advantage of the exceptional countryside surrounding it. If you stray from the village in any direction there are focus points for climbing and hiking. Oh, and if it's not too chilly try taking a dip in the open air swimming pool.

Length	**6.4km/4miles**
Allow	**2 hours**
Terrain	**Good paths across farmland and through woods. A small section of road at the start and end**

Refreshments	**Conveniently, near the start and end of this walk, there is a great place to get a bite to eat. As you walk down the main road from the station, you'll pass the famous David Mellor cutlery shop and it's worth popping in to check out the shop and the café. Alternatively, from the station extend the walk into Hathersage village. At the end of the road, just before the junction, there is a café on the left called Elliots that welcomes walkers. You can get a good selection of food and drinks at this popular pit stop**
Getting there	**Hathersage is easy to reach by road. The village lies on the A6187 road between Hope and Calver, south west of Sheffield. Once there, follow the signs for the station, which lies off the B6001. Getting a train to Hathersage takes an hour from Manchester and 18 minutes from Sheffield. Grid reference SK 232, 810**
Next stations	**South east of Hathersage, the next station is Grindleford, while you'll find Bamford up the tracks to the north west**
Map	**OS Outdoor Leisure 01 Dark Peak Area**

Route

From Hathersage Railway Station, walk to the main B6001 road and turn left onto it. There are paths to walk off the road. Keep going past the cutlery centre and just before you get to the bridge there is a path off to the left signed for Grindleford. The path has the River Derwent on the right and soon bends round to the right.

As you approach a house, the path heads through a gate on the right and into a field. Continue across the grassy fields with the river on your right until you pass through a gate and enter Coppice Wood. When the path forks in two, stick to the right and continue close to the river until you leave Coppice Wood. You're now out onto fields once more and you carry on walking by the river.

As you walk by the river, your route will eventually become blocked by a fence and at this point you turn left and walk alongside it. Soon you go over a stile and come to a bridge going over Burbage Brook.

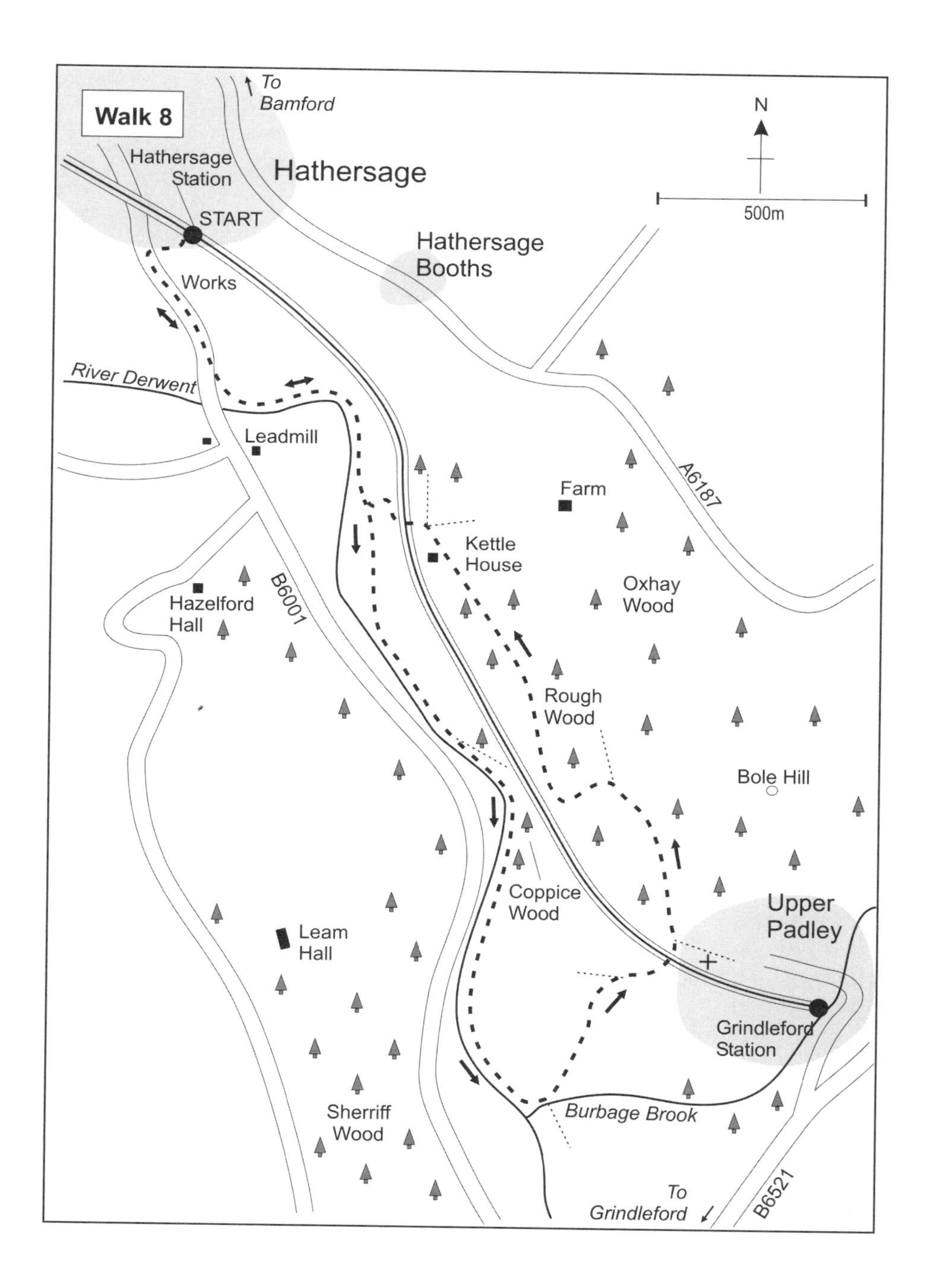
Walk 8
To Bamford
Hathersage
Hathersage Station
START
N
500m
Hathersage Booths
Works
River Derwent
Leadmill
Farm
A6187
Kettle House
Hazelford Hall
B6001
Oxhay Wood
Rough Wood
Bole Hill
Coppice Wood
Upper Padley
Leam Hall
Grindleford Station
Sherriff Wood
Burbage Brook
To Grindleford
B6521

The path leads you alongside te River Derwent

Don't go across the bridge, instead turn left and enter the field, keeping the dry stone wall on your left. Follow this wall until you pass into another field, at which point you need to veer right and aim for the middle of the wall at the other side. Leave the field, turning right onto a track and cross over the train track.

Once across the bridge, go through a gate and turn right onto a track past some houses. Go past a wood on your right and look out for the wall on your right ending; at that point, turn left and go down the grassy bank, following signs for the Derwent Valley Heritage Way. Head towards another bridge but before you reach it, turn right onto a track through the wood. You're now in Rough Wood and you have a decent walk through here before coming out at a farm. Continue ahead across a field and when the path splits in two turn left and go under the railway. Carry on until you meet the path at the bottom and turn right onto it. This will bring you out once again at the B6001 road, where you should turn right and head up under the bridge and look out for the station entrance on your right.

Walk 9
Bamford

A beautiful amble by the upper reaches of the River Derwent, stretching onto the moors and back through fields to the idyllic village of Thornhill.

Bamford Station

Opened in June 1894, Bamford had a manned railway station right up until 1969 when the last Station Master to operate there bought the station house to live in. The former station building has now been demolished, but the station continues to operate and is used by 24,000 passengers a year. The station took on special significance in the early 20th century when a branch line was built from near the station and

Bamford railway station in 1966 *(photograph © Ben Brooksbank)*

headed up the valley to where workers were constructing the Derwent and Howden Reservoirs. This was crucial for transporting stone from a quarry in Grindleford. Although the branch line was taken up after the reservoirs were complete, it was laid again in the 1940s as Ladybower Reservoir was built. This walk takes you along part of this disused branch line once so important in securing a water supply for nearby cities.

Hope Valley Line

One of the most scenic lines in the country, The Hope Valley Line connects Sheffield with Manchester and stops along the way at some delightful villages. The line branches off the Midland Main Line at Dore, heads through the Totley tunnel and calls at Grindleford, Hathersage, Bamford, Hope, Edale, Chinley and joins the line to Manchester via New Mills. Beyond Chinley, southern branch loops off to join the line to Buxton and Stockport. Trains running along this line today are operated by Northern Rail, East Midlands Trains, and TransPennine Express.

The line that connects Dore with Chinley across this section of the Pennines was not the first proposal to bridge the gap between Sheffield and Manchester. Back in 1872, you would have had to make the journey via Ambergate and then head along the newly built line via Monsal Dale. The first idea was to develop a line from Dore to Hassop to have the Sheffield trains meet the line to Manchester here, but the more direct route to meet the Manchester line in Chinley was given the green light in 1884. Four years later, work began on this challenging route to negotiate some of the trickiest territory that had been attempted on a train line. Despite being only 21 miles long, the railway link had some difficult terrain to overcome, including the Totley and Cowburn Tunnels.

Ladybower Reservoir

You are approaching the halfway point of the walk when you reach Ladybower Reservoir and it's quite fitting that the Thornhill Trail route you have followed is the former railway that brought locally quarried stone up to Derwent Valley, which now houses three dam walls. Ladybower Reservoir was the last of the three to be built and construction took place between 1935 and 1943, though it took another two years for it to fill with water. In 1945 it was opened officially by King George VI, accompanied by Queen Elizabeth.

Length	6.5km/4miles
Allow	2 hours 20 minutes
Terrain	The paths on the outward route are easy to follow, with those on the return section being steep in places and at times a little muddy
Refreshments	Although there are no refreshments available directly on the route, a good pub meal can be bought at the nearby Yorkshire Bridge. It's on the A6013, close to Ladybower Reservoir. Grid Reference SK 201, 851
Getting there	Bamford Railway Station lies to the south of the village of Bamford at grid reference SK 208, 825. Just off the A6013, the station is close to the junction with the A6187. There is a free car park here. By train, the journey time from Manchester is 52 minutes and from Sheffield it is a 26 minute trip
Next stations	Hope lies to the north west and Hathersage is along the line to the south east
Map	OS Outdoor Leisure 01 Dark Peak Area

Route

From the station car park, walk down the lane to the main A6013 road and turn right onto it. Walk on the path by the side of the road until you see Water Lane off to the left and a sign for Bamford Tennis Club. Continue down the lane, passing an old Derwent Valley Water Board building on the right, now owned by the Quaker Community. Beyond the house, turn right onto the path signed for Yorkshire Bridge and Thornhill. Going through a gate, you are now on the Thornhill Trail which is the route of the old train line that took quarried stone up to the dam sites. With great views opening up on the right, this route takes you past a decorative stone and soon after that you have to cross a road, picking up the trail again at the other side. You'll soon see the grassy bank of the dam wall on the right and come to a concrete track, onto which you need to turn left.

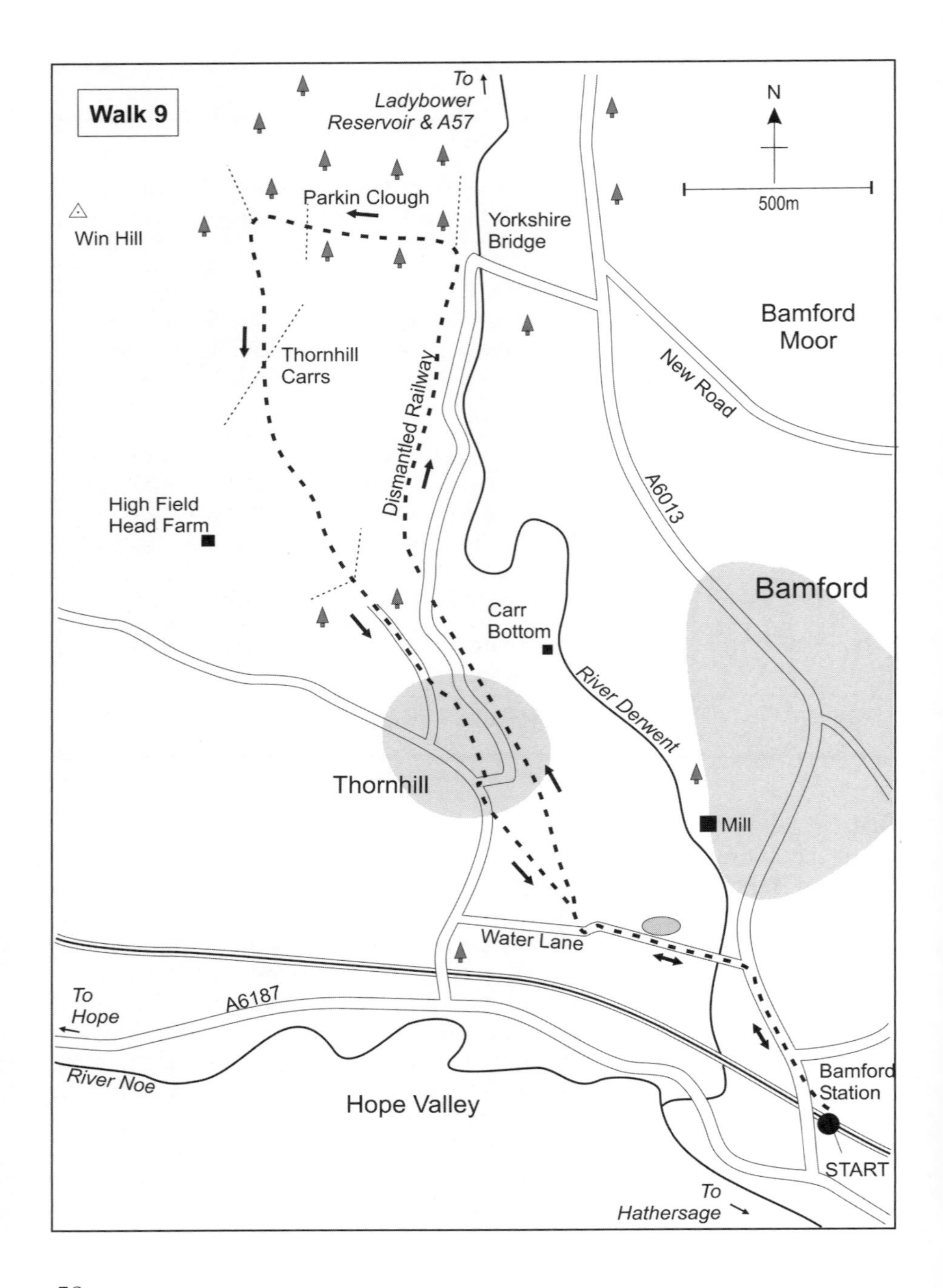
Walk 9
To Ladybower Reservoir & A57
N
500m
Parkin Clough
Win Hill
Yorkshire Bridge
Bamford Moor
New Road
Thornhill Carrs
Dismantled Railway
A6013
High Field Head Farm
Bamford
Carr Bottom
River Derwent
Thornhill
Mill
Water Lane
To Hope
A6187
River Noe
Hope Valley
Bamford Station
START
To Hathersage

An elevated view of Ladybower Reservoir

The path now runs alongside Ladybower Reservoir and when the A6013 road bridge comes into view, look out for a track running up the hill to the left. Take this, go through the gate and begin to climb into the woods. You will soon see a path that crosses the track and you need to head left onto the smaller route through the trees. Continue along this, ignoring other paths off to the left and right. Eventually you'll come to Parkin Clough, which is one of the main routes up to the top of Win Hill, which lies up to the right. Cross over the stream at this point and continue straight ahead. Shortly after you leave the woods and enter the moors, with superb open views on the left.

After walking through the ferns for some time, your path joins another, larger path and you should turn left onto it. Soon after, as you approach a dry stone wall, head down to the left and join a path heading down to the left. Follow this track as it takes you down towards Thornhill, when you see some buildings in front of you. On reaching the buildings, continue ahead onto the road, and turn left when you reach the T-junction. This will bring you out at another junction with a telephone box on the corner, and you should turn right here.

Soon after, take the track on the left and follow it until it brings out at the Thornhill Trail once more. Turn right onto it until the trail ends, and then turn left past the old Water Board building. This turns into the track that crosses the river and brings you out to the A6013. Turn right onto this road and watch out for the road heading off to the railway station on your left, which is where your walk began.

Walk 10
Hope

The farming fields around Hope are the setting for this walk, with the wonderful hills of the Hope Valley towering above. Cross under the rails via old bridges on a circular route to Hope Station, which is just outside the village of Hope.

Hope station

Built in 1894, the station where this walk starts from was once called Hope Village but it was renamed Hope in 1974. That was probably because it's not just a station for Hope village, but also serves a large section of the Hope Valley, including nearby villages Brough, Bradwell and Castleton. The station lies to the east of Hope and if you're catching a

Rolling countryside of Hope Valley

train to Manchester from here you immediately head through some amazing scenery as the line passes directly between Win Hill and Lose Hill. Shortly after leaving Hope, there is a short branch line which allows freight trains to arc round and call in at the cement works to the south of the village.

Hope

I've had a connection with Hope since being a young lad because my dad used to work at the cement works, a plant which dominates the surroundings and can be seen from miles away when you are atop any of the nearby hills. A controversial structure, critics must remember that the tall chimney and associated building was constructed before the Peak District was a national park and that, although lying on the border between the white and dark peak, there are several more cement works in the Peak District. There is more to Hope than cement and the rumblings of articulated lorries, however, although it has to be said that many tourists bypass the village on their way to Castleton. Those that do make a point of stopping at Hope are often in search of the annual Well Dressing, where the local water source is decorated with a magnificent design of flower petals. Other visitors head for the parish church which houses two ancient crosses, one of which was hidden in the village school from the time of the Civil War until 1858. There are over 900 people which call Hope their home, as do the Edale Mountain Rescue team which is based at the cement works.

Origins of Hope

There are a variety of different rock types visible from the Hope Valley, each of which gives an insight into the region's history. The white limestone seen over at Winnats Pass is a reminder of when this part of the country was close to the equator and under a tropical sea 350 million years ago. The limestone was formed from millions of dead sea creatures that dropped to the bottom of the sea and was compressed into stone over time. The fossils are a clue to this past, but there is evidence from other times as well. Some 50 million years later, a river flowed over this region and had its source in what is now the north of Scotland. The sediment this river brought with it was compressed and formed the shale which now forms part of Mam Tor. Elsewhere, sand and pebbles were compressed to form the harder Millstone Grit, which can be seen on the various 'edges' around Hope and was utilised to make millstones in local industry.

Length	5km/3.1miles
Allow	1 hour 40 minutes
Terrain	Good paths, a small section of road walking, some steady inclines and one sharp descent
Refreshments	No cafés or pubs are passed on the route, but there is a good selection of places to grab a bite to eat or a drink in Hope after the walk. A good place to start is the Cheshire Cheese Inn on Edale Road, which has good meals, real ales and rooms if you want to stop over
Getting there	Hope Railway Station is found around a mile to the east of the village of Hope on the A6187. The turning for the station is off the main road before you reach the village, and is located west of the junction with the A6013. Grid reference SK 180, 832. Trains to Hope take 54 minutes from Manchester and 27 minutes from Sheffield
Next stations	Bamford station is the next station along the line to south east, while Edale lies up the tracks to the north west
Map	OS Outdoor Leisure 01 Dark Peak Area

Route

From the station, go over the footbridge to the other side of the tracks and take the footpath straight ahead that bends round to the right. Head through the gate and go across the field, crossing over the stile and entering the other field at the end. On this stretch of the walk you'll be able to see Mam Tor away to the left as you walk by the stream on your right, with the cement works looming behind you. Underneath the electricity wires, you head through a gate and continue ahead through the fields and a small wood before reaching the road at Aston. Here, you turn left onto the road and then immediately right.

Climb up the road and at the top, where you reach a house, take the track off to the left which is signed as a footpath. Keep on this route heading through a gate and eventually finding a ruined building on the right. Heading through another gate, keep an eye out for the intersection of footpaths (grid reference SK 178, 847) and turn left down the steep hill. Go beyond Twitchill Farm on the track and head down to the train line. Once there, the track bends round to the right and then veers left under a bridge.

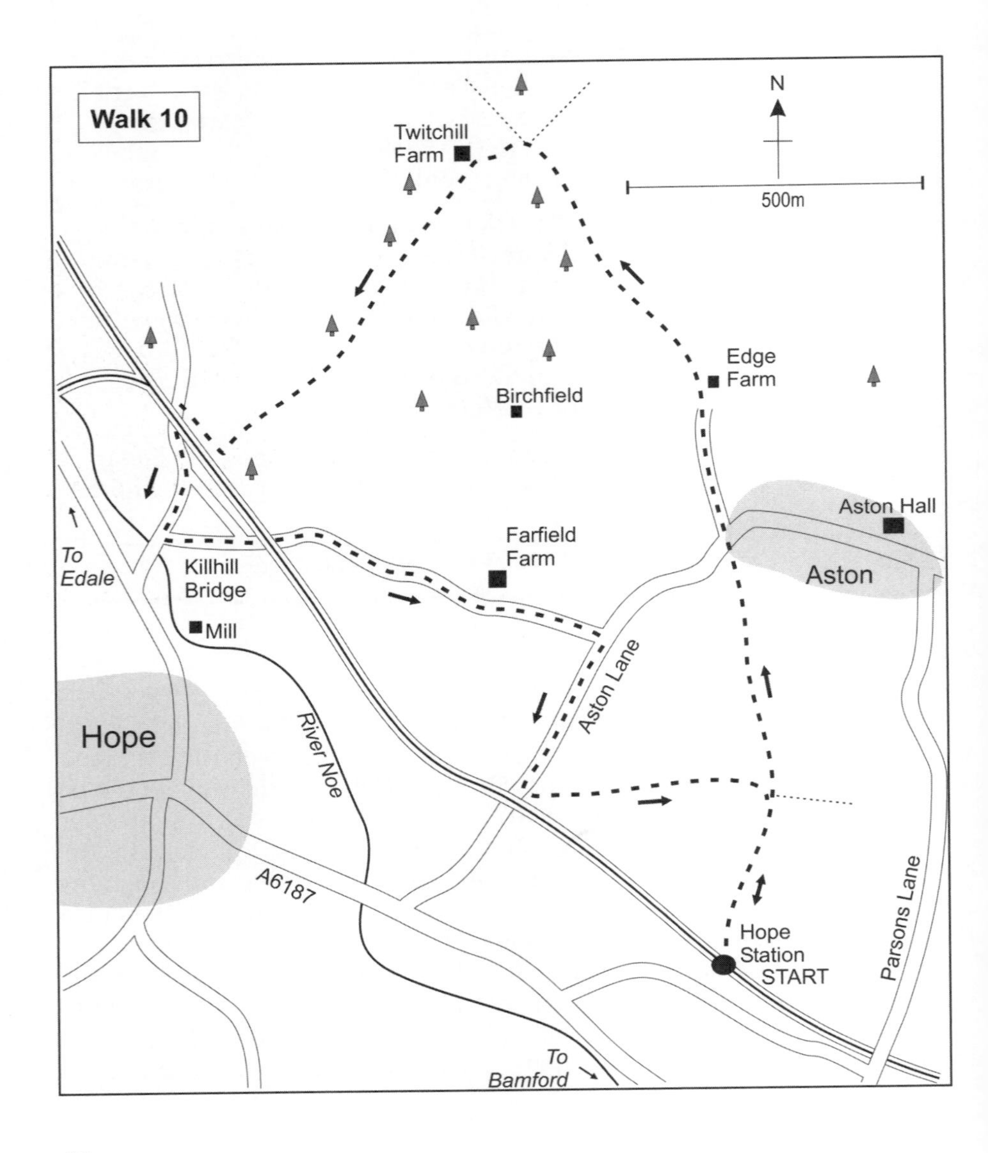

A ruined farm building in the Hope Valley

You'll soon see a path off to the left, which you should take, and go past the cemetery on your left. This takes you under another bridge and the path then bends to the right and takes you through a farm and campsite. Turn right onto the road and just before you reach the train track once again, take the path off to the left. Cross over three fields and then turn right onto the path that takes you back down to the train station. Go through the gate, follow the path round and cross over the footbridge to reach the starting point.

Walk 11
Edale

A lovely walk through tiny hamlets close to Edale, around the head of the Vale of Edale and back along the Pennine Way.

Edale Station

Opened in 1894, this is one of the more remote stations in the Peak District and has the stunning backdrop of Kinder Scout to make its setting extremely atmospheric. Orignally a manned station, Edale has been unstaffed since 1969 and today has over 60,000 people using it every year. Many of these passengers are heading to Edale from Manchester and Sheffield to enjoy a hike in the Derbyshire hills. Indeed, some may be making a one-way journey to Edale and setting out on the Pennine Way, which starts in the nearby village. This lengthy, famous route winds along a tricky route some 267 miles to the north, ending up in Kirk Yeholm, Scotland. But if you are leaving from Edale, make sure you know which platform you need before you head for it. There is no level crossing or bridge to get across the rails and the only way to get to the other side is to head back down to the main road, under the bridge and up the other side.

From Edale Station, the line heads to the head of the Vale of Edale and disappears into the hillside through the Cowburn Tunnel. At 3,385 metres long, this tunnel that cuts a way through the Peak District moorland was opened in 1891 and is hugely significant in that it helps provide the only rail link across the hills from Sheffield to Manchester. Unlike most tunnels, it was not engineered to keep a constant gradient underground; the highest point of the Hope Valley Line is actually inside the tunnel.

The Pennine Way

There's weeks of adventures laying north of Edale on the Pennine Way. Although this picturesque village is the start of this long and historic route, the real fun starts when you leave Edale and head onto the tops of Kinder Scout, and beyond to Bleaklow, the Yorkshire Dales and Northumberland. In fact, this long distance path which leaves the heart of the Peak District will have you in Scotland in 16 days time - perhaps a few days longer if you want to build in some rest time.

The Pennine Way, all 268 miles of it, is sandwiched between two pubs, the first being The Nagg's Head at Edale and the finishing post (if you are walking south to north, as most do) is the Border Inn at Kirk Yetholm. Well over half the walk is within designated national parks, making it a stunning long distance walk to complete, with the highest point being Cross Fell some 893 metres above sea level. The idea for this lengthy path that runs along the backbone of the country was the brainchild of writer and rambler Tom Stephenson. He proposed the idea and lobbied Parliament from 1935, eventually seeing the full route designated as the Pennine Way in 1965. The biggest drawback of the path is the weather; you are unlikely to get three weeks in this part of the world without encountering rain, mist, fog or some other uncomfortably atmospheric condition. Good luck to those who attempt it!

Length	**8.3km/5.1miles**
Allow	**3 hours 15 minutes**
Terrain	**Some steep climbs and descents, along well used routes**
Refreshments	**Just down from the station car park, there is a National Trust café called The Penny Pot which serves good quality food and drink. Tel: 01433 670293**
Getting there	**Edale does not sit on a main road, so look out for the small turnings that lead to the village. From Hope to the east on the A6187, the turning to Edale can be found opposite the church in the middle of the village. Coming from the west, take the road signed for Castleton from either Chinley or Chapel-en-le-Frith and before you reach Winnats Pass there will be a road turning off for Edale. The train to Edale takes 35 minutes from Sheffield and if you're coming from Manchester Picadilly it will be a 45 minute trip. There is a pay and display car park at the entrance to the village and also at the train station. Grid reference: SK 123, 853**
Next stations	**Chinley lies to the south west, with Hope being the next station to the south east**
Map	**OS Outdoor Leisure 01 Dark Peak Area**

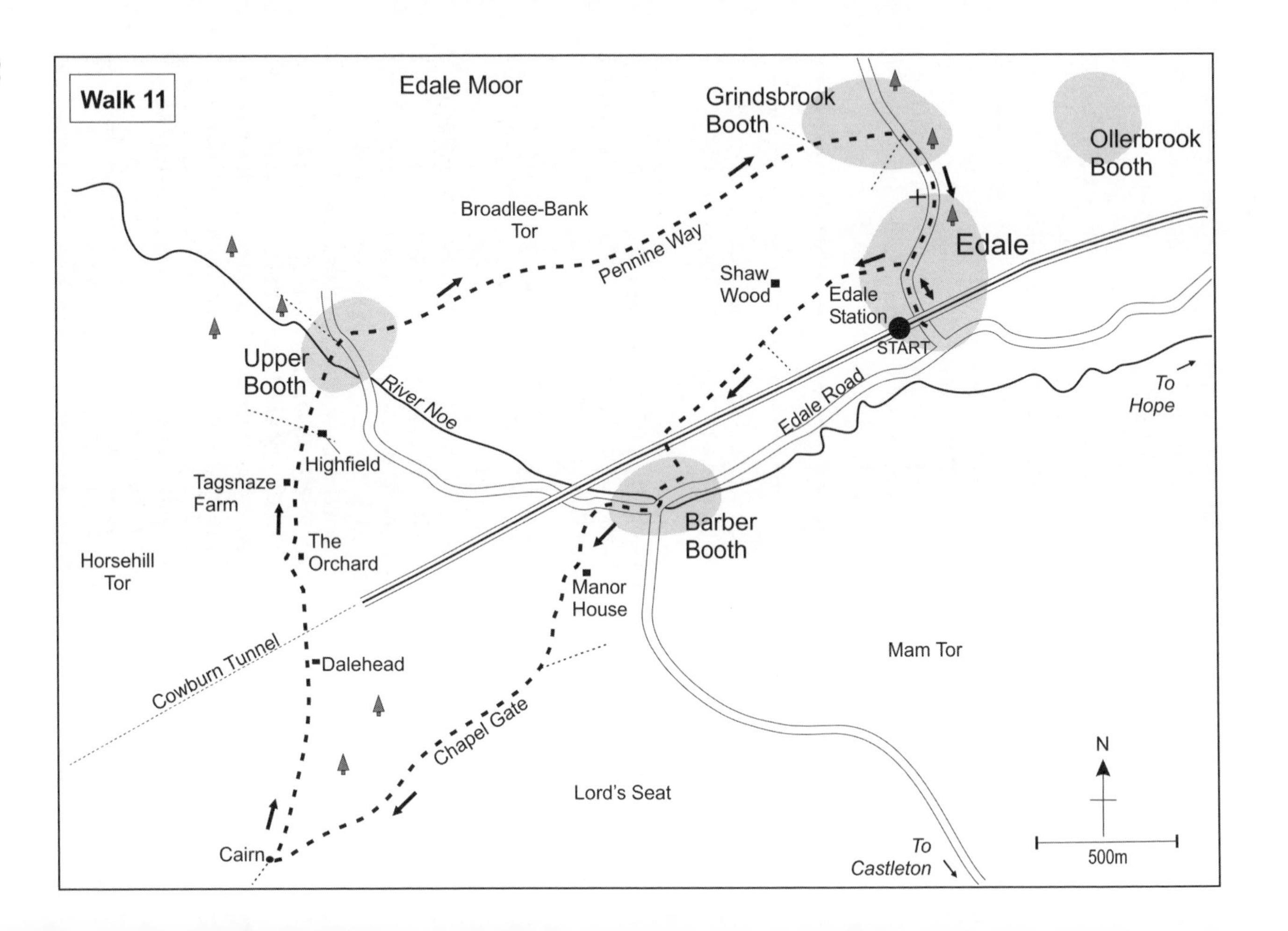
Walk 11
Edale Moor
Grindsbrook Booth
Ollerbrook Booth
Broadlee-Bank Tor
Pennine Way
Edale
Shaw Wood
Edale Station
START
Upper Booth
River Noe
Edale Road
To Hope
Highfield
Tagsnaze Farm
Barber Booth
The Orchard
Horsehill Tor
Manor House
Mam Tor
Cowburn Tunnel
Dalehead
Chapel Gate
Lord's Seat
N
Cairn
To Castleton
500m

Route

From the train station car park, head down the road past the Penny Pot Café. Turn left onto the main road and head beyond The Rambler Inn, enjoying views of Kinder Scout ahead of you. As the road bends to the right, take the path on the left which heads past a house and into a series of fields. With Mam Tor up away to the left, cross the fields and then head over a stream, where the footpath bears off to the left. Head past a farm building on your right and follow signs across the fields for Upper Booth via Barber Booth. The path takes you down towards the train line, where on your right you get a great view of the head of the valley.

There is a path which takes you left on a bridge over the railway. When you reach the road at Barber Booth, turn right and follow the sign for Upper Booth. Continue down along the road, crossing a bridge and taking a road on the right signed for Upper Booth. Take the path on the left you soon come across and half way through the first field cross over the stream. When this path comes out at a track, cross over it and head into the field opposite. At the other side of the field is a stile, turn left immediately after it and follow the path by the fence. Continue along this

Looking towards the Cowburn Tunnel from Edale

One of the many streams running down from the moors around Edale

path, heading up through different fields, until you reach a large gate leading onto a track. This is called Chapel Gate and you turn right onto it and follow it up the hill.

When you reach the brow of the hill, you can clearly see a footpath sign piercing the skyline. Turn right here, following path 98 by Dalehead towards Upper Booth and Hayfield. This path takes you all the way down the hill, with the valley looking splendid to the right. Cross a small footbridge over Whitemoor Clough and follow the footpath signs at the other side until you reach a house at Dalehead. Turn right on the track before the house, but immediately after it take the path on the left, heading over the footbridge.

Follow the footpath past the air vent for the tunnel, and cross the stiles between the fields to a farm on the right. Continue across the fields until you reach another farm. When you get here, make your way to the ruined building at the far side and from here take the path over the wall to Upper Booth. Head past the big tree in the field, enter the woods beyond it and head down to the footbridge before continuing up to Upper Booth. Once there, follow the signs for the Pennine Way and Edale. When you enter the farm and go onto the track, make sure you take the sign clearly marked with the Pennine Way symbol towards Edale.

This is a very well used path that is the start (or end) of the Pennine Way and takes you across plenty of fields on the final mile. Keep following the route for the Pennine Way and Edale. When you eventually reach the village, turn right onto the main road and carry on until you see the train station on your right.

Walk 12
Chinley

An historical journey to Cracken Edge past old quarry workings.

Chinley Station

Like most of the railway stations in the Peak District, Chinley's glory days lay in the past. But at least the trains still stop here, and at last count there were in excess of 100,000 people using this island platform on the main line between Sheffield and Manchester. Some of these will be for hikers wanting to the explore the hills to the west of Kinder that feature on this route. Others, though, use Chinley to commute into Manchester. It is, after all, a little over 17 miles to the city centre.

At its height, Chinley was an important junction between the major cities of Manchester, Sheffield and London; trains left here for the capital after an extension was built south towards New Mills. In 1902 there were five platforms here and a new station was built to replace the original that

The hills around Chinley have a history of quarrying

in 1867. It was common for people to change trains here when completing their long distance routes.

The importance of Chinley as a former junction can be understood when making your way here and you see the range of embankments and viaducts surrounding the village. But when the line heading south was closed in 1967, one hundred years after trains first stopped here, the significance of Chinley took a turn for the worse. Today there is one island platform, with a track running on either side. Trains running between Manchester and Sheffield stop here roughly once an hour in peak times, once every two hours otherwise.

The railway has had, and still does have, an important role in the development of the village, which now houses 2,000 people. Before engines chugged through, there was an overwhelming dependency on agriculture. But mills were built locally when it became easier to get materials – and staff – in and out. The railway is still important today to allow people to commute to their service jobs in nearby cities.

Length	8.2km/5.1miles
Allow	3 hours
Terrain	Good paths and some walking on a quiet road. Inclines can be steep, with one path being fairly thin and at the side of a big drop
Refreshments	With no places to stop on the actual route, it's important to have somewhere to look forward to at the end of the walk. Heading out of Chinley for the A6 from the A624, you'll see The Fallow Deer pub on your left, serving a range of meals. Tel: 01298 812346. www.fallowdeerpub.co.uk For those coming in on the train, there is a shop on the main street to pick up snacks
Getting there	The train station at Chinley sits just a few metres from the National Park boundary at grid reference SK 038, 826. You can reach the start of this walk by getting the train here, with the journey time being 27 minutes from Manchester and 40 minutes from Sheffield. By car, you'll find Chinley just off the A6 between Chapel-en-le-Frith and Whaley Bridge.

Getting there (cont'd)	**Follow the signs off here for Chinley and, from the centre of the village, you'll see signs for the train station. The car park is on the right just before you reach the station**
Next stations	**New Mills and Hazel Grove lay on the Manchester bound track, with Edale being the next stop heading for Sheffield**
Map	**OS Outdoor Leisure 01 Dark Peak Area**

Route

From the station, walk back on the road towards the centre of the village and then turn right. Head past Green Lane and cross the railway bridge towards the war memorial. Turn left and continue up this road, following it round to the right when there is a turning to Cote Bank. Soon after you will see a mast off to the right and you take a footpath on the right immediately after it. This track climbs uphill with steep banks on either side. Take the track off to the left towards Cracken Edge. The path you are heading on makes its way towards a farm, but just before you reach it there is a path off to the right.

Across the first field, head up three little steps to a gate and then take the path as it turns off to the left. At the top of this incline, go through a gate and follow the path straight ahead and then round to the right. There are some great views off to the right at this stage, towards Kinder Scout, and ahead of you is a stile you need to climb over. Look out for the old quarry transporter on the right and then stick to the narrow path as it climbs steadily upwards and, when it levels out, goes by some interesting old quarry workings.

Ahead of you on the right you will be able to see a farm building; follow the path as it eases a way down towards it. After passing it, go through a gate and head through a farmer's field before joining a track you need to turn left onto. Go past Hills Farm, heading through a gateway and continuing on ahead. When you reach the brow of the hill, a stunning view of Manchester opens up in front of you. On a clear day you will be able to pick out the city centre, Welsh mountains, wind farms near Bolton, Jodrell Bank and Fiddlers Ferry Power Station.

When you reach a junction of paths, continue straight ahead on the bridleway. The track has walls on both sides enclosing it, but eventually

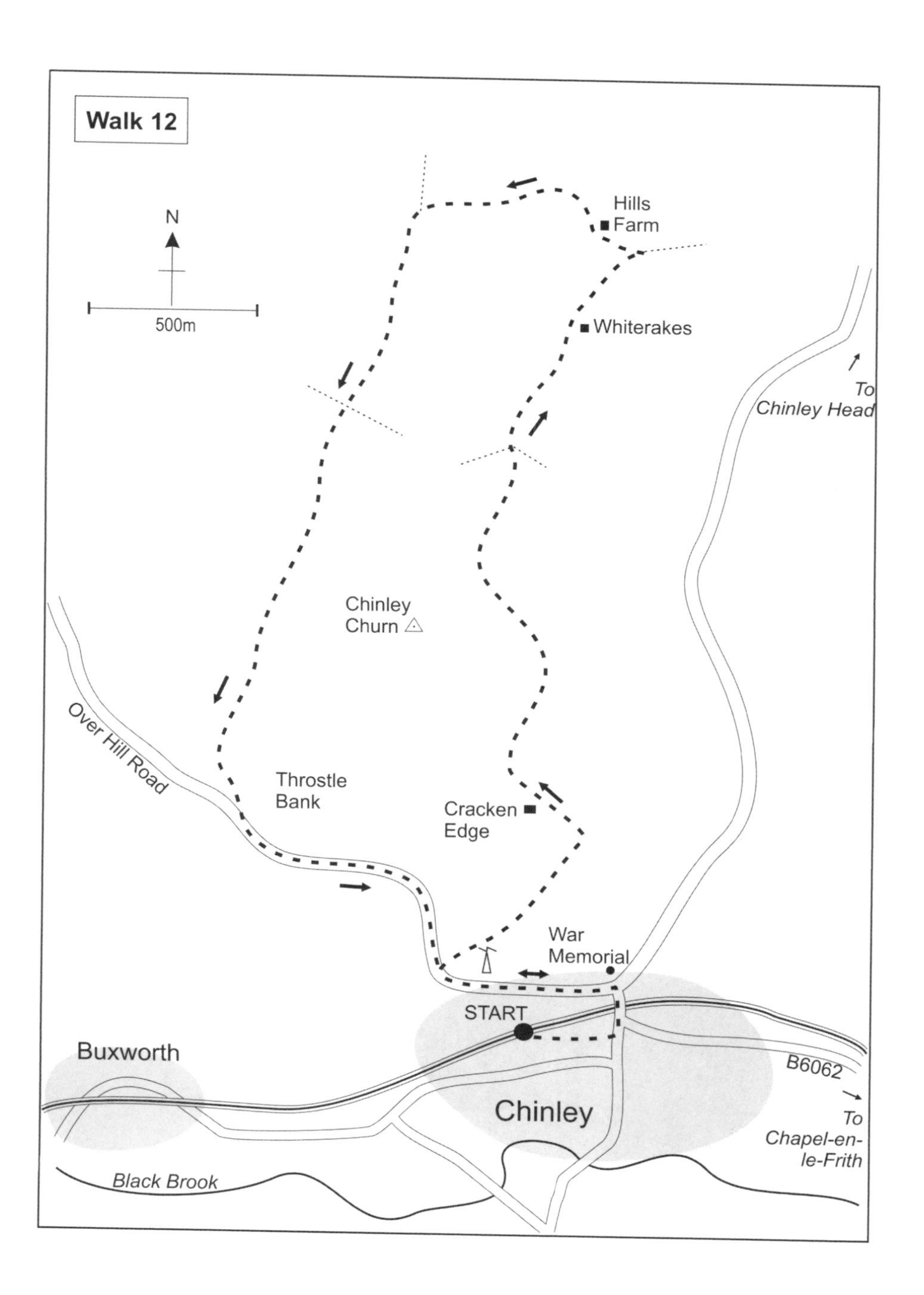
Walk 12
N
500m
Hills
Farm
Whiterakes
To
Chinley Head
Chinley
Churn
Over Hill Road
Throstle
Bank
Cracken
Edge
War
Memorial
START
Buxworth
B6062
Chinley
To
Chapel-en-
le-Frith
Black Brook

you enter a field. At the next interchange of paths go straight ahead, again on a bridleway. Continue through a series of gates as the path heads gently downhill, eventually bringing you out at a road. Turn left onto this and stick to it until it brings you back to the war memorial. Turn right here across the bridge and take the first right towards to the railway station.

Old quarry workings at Cracken Edge

Walk 13
Hadfield

The urban station of Hadfield makes way for the Longdendale Trail, following the route of the old railway.

Hadfield Station

A busy commuter station serving somewhere in the region of 315,000 passengers a year, Hadfield Station is still very much in use today. The line coming out of Manchester, however, once ran far beyond Hadfield, past Crowden, through the Woodhead Tunnel and on to Wath and Sheffield. Passenger services stopped going further than Hadfield in 1970, though, and when freight stopped in the early 1980s the line was soon taken up. The abrupt ending of the Manchester to Glossop line serves as a reminder that trains were once given access to the rolling countryside side that lies above Hadfield, further reminders of the area's railway history can be found all along the Longdendale Trail that follows the route. The Manchester to Glossop Line forks in two just before reaching its easternmost point and today Hadfield Station forms one of the two termini that lay at the foothills of the Pennines, the other being neighbouring Glossop itself.

Hadfield

Nestling at the foothills of the Peak District and with the train line still allowing commuters to reach Manchester, Hadfield is an important settlement on the edge of the countryside. Most people pass by on either the Woodhead or Snake Pass without popping in. But Hadfield is known to many who haven't even been to the area because it is the setting for Royston Vasey, the odd town at the heart of TV show *The League Of Gentlemen.* Fans will be able to point out several filming locations if they visit, but Hadfield also appeared as itself in *The League of Gentlemen's Apocalypse*, when the characters entered the real world through a portal at the church. You're unlikely to see anything so exciting if you go for a wander round, but there are a range of shops to keep you busy if you're waiting for your train to arrive.

The Longdendale Trail

Following the closure of the Woodhead Line, this former public transport route went through the same transformation as the Monsal Trail and the Tissington Trail. The gentle gradients and potential for smooth, wide paths make this an ideal route for walkers and cyclists. It was good to see the Longdendale Trail opening up for recreation in 1992, allowing access to the section between the former Woodhead Station and Hadfield, a distance just shy of 7 miles. The Longdendale Trail also forms part of the Trans Pennine Trail which crosses the country between Hornsea and Southport, a total of 207 miles which makes the small section of the Longdendale Trail minuscule in comparison. Ideas surrounding the Trans Pennine Trail first emerged in 1987 and aimed to use as many old train lines as possible. The result is not just the east to west route across the Pennines, but several spurs off it, including a north-south route from Leeds to Chesterfield and a separate diversion to York.

Length	**4.8km/2.9miles**
Allow	**1 hour 15 minutes**
Terrain	**Well established paths with a few gentle slopes**
Refreshments	**A stroll down Station Road in Hadfield will offer you a range of places to eat and drink, including Dolly's Café. Tel: 0145 7 867643. Follow them on Twitter @dollyshadfield**
Getting there	**Hadfield is to be found at the western end of the A628 Woodhead Pass. From both the villages of Tintwistle and Hollingworth you will signs for Hadfield and it's only a short distance from there. Head for the train station, but for free parking you may think it better to drive past the station and base yourself at the Longdendale Trail car park (grid reference SK 025, 961). By train, Hadfield takes around 40 minutes from Manchester Piccadilly**
Next stations	**The train used to climb the hill to Crowden, but there is still train from Hadfield Station in the other direction. The next stop on the way to Manchester is Dinting**
Map	**OS Outdoor Leisure 01 Dark Peak Area**

Route

For those starting at the train station in Hadfield, head down to the road and turn right onto it, following the signs for the Longdendale Trail. Soon you will see the free car park on your left, which is another good starting point for the walk. From this car park, climb the short path to the trail and begin walking on the route of the old Woodhead Line. Trains haven't been seen on here for several decades, but the remnants of the historic transport system are still there and you will soon go underneath an old railway bridge that carries Padfield Main Road above.

Heading underneath th Longdendale Trail

Keep going until you reach a footpath sign, which sends you off to the right following directions for the Trans Pennine Trail West. This path takes you around the corner and down under the bridge that carries the Longdendale Trail you were just walking on. As you emerge onto the other side, you'll see a field in front of you with Bottoms Reservoir on the left. Go through the gate and head across the field, aiming for the far right hand side, following signs for TPT West again. You'll find yourself down on the path that goes around the reservoir and you should turn right here and head towards Valehouse.

The trail runs from Woodhead to Hadfield

Take the path off to the left that goes across the dam wall.

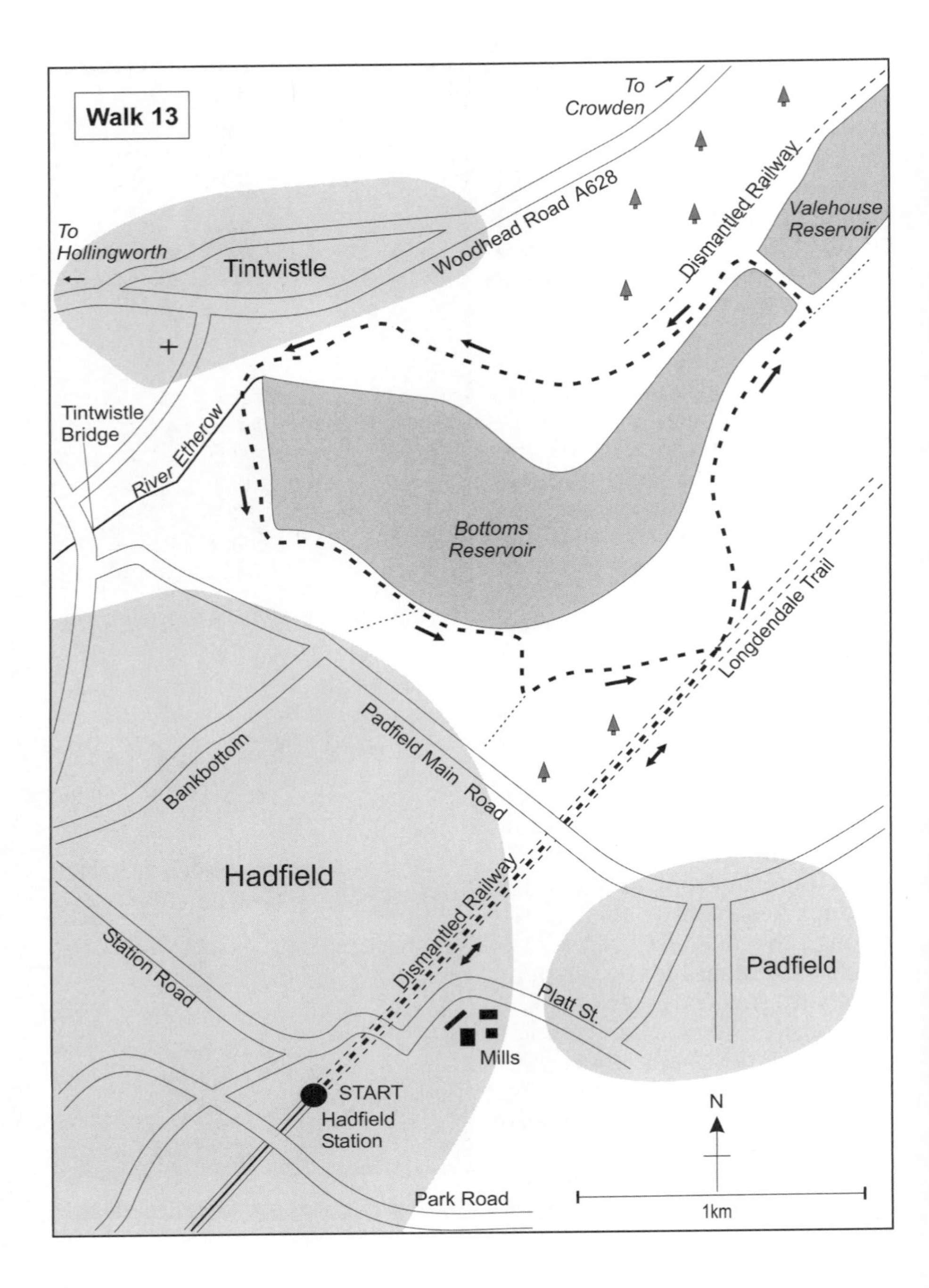
Walk 13
To Crowden
To Hollingworth
Tintwistle
Woodhead Road A628
Dismantled Railway
Valehouse Reservoir
Tintwistle Bridge
River Etherow
Bottoms Reservoir
Longdendale Trail
Padfield Main Road
Bankbottom
Hadfield
Dismantled Railway
Station Road
Platt St.
Padfield
Mills
START
Hadfield Station
N
Park Road
1km

Here the route enjoys great views of the expanses of water and surrounding hills, with Bottoms Reservoir on the left and Valehouse Reservoir on the right. At the end of the dam wall, follow the concessionary footpath that sticks close to the water's edge. When this path ends, go through the gate and take the path opposite, with the water channel on your right. Follow the path around to the left when you reach the overflow and you will make your way to the corner of the dam wall, where you should turn left and walk straight along the path.

When you reach the end, another left turn is needed as you once again walk close to the reservoir with the water on your left. Ignore the first path signed off for Hadfield, but when you reach the second one, go through the gate and turn right onto the path up the hill. You'll soon come to a junction of paths and you should turn left here, making your way to the far right corner of the field. Follow the path over the fields and you will soon see the Longdendale Trail off to the right. Take the path to the right and go under the bridge you went through earlier in the walk. When you bend round up to the Longdendale Trail, turn left onto it and continue straight ahead until you reach the end. Take the path down to the right to reach the Longdendale Trail car park. If you parked at the actual train station, go towards the road, turn right onto it and follow it round until you reach the starting point.

Bottoms Reservoir is one of several alongside the Longdendale Trail

Walk 14
Crowden

Nestled high in the hills on the Woodhead Pass, Crowden is a wonderful place to escape the hustle and bustle of city life. It's hard to imagine what Crowden was like when it had its own train station, but signs of the past can still be spotted at the station thanks to the line's coversion to a popular cycle path.

Crowden Station

The station at the start of this walk was given the name Crowden, but actually sits some distance away from the small hamlet of the same name. Crowden can be found on the Woodhead Pass, and today most people simply speed by it on the way to Sheffield or Manchester. Those stopping can enjoy good walks in the area and stop over at a Youth Hostel, but there is little else to do. Many people staying at the Youth Hostel have walked into Crowden from Edale, for this is the first major stopping point on the Pennine Way. Back in 1844 when the Woodhead Line was opened, there were again few people stopping off at Crowden because the trains also steamed by. It was not until a local mill owner donated £50 to the cause in 1857 that the train company even considered placing a station at Crowden. Even then, a stop was not built and the donation was not returned. When the mill owner complained in 1860 about the loss of money, the plan was drawn up again and this time the building work commenced. The station was opened in 1861, closing in 1958 - some thirteen years before the last passenger service trundled through the hills.

Length	**7km/4.3miles**
Allow	**2 hours**
Terrain	**Mainly on good, level paths. Some uneven ground on the north side of the reservoir and steps to climb to get back to the starting point**
Refreshments	**None on the route, but if you're heading east after the walk try the Dog and Partridge on the A628 (01226 763173 www.dogandpartridgeinn.co.uk) or, to the west, The Gun at Hollingworth (01457 762388)**

Getting there	**The settlement of Crowden lies some way away from the former railway station, sitting on the A628 Woodhead Pass between Tintwistle and Langsett. On the Langsett side of Crowden, a small road heads off between the reservoirs. This is the B6105, which you should take. Just before the road bends round to the right at the end of the dam wall, there are some parking spaces on the left (grid reference SK 081, 993). If there is no room here, continue on the road and use Torside Car Park (SK 068, 983), meaning you will have to join the circular route further down**
Next stations	**East of here the trains ran up to Woodhead, and to the south west the next station was Hadfield, which is still in use**
Map	**OS Outdoor Leisure 01 Dark Peak Area**

Route

From the site of the former Crowden Railway Station, join the Longdendale Trail and head west, gradually downhill towards Manchester, following signs for Hadfield. The trail gradually angles off to the left and so moves away from Torside Reservoir. Moving into woods, the trees blocks the view of the reservoir, but it will feature in the walk again soon.

Before long, the path is broken up by a couple of gates and a track leading down to the Torside car park. If you have had to park here, this is where you pick up the road. Continue down the Longdendale Trail towards Hadfield. Before long, you come to a road and should carefully cross over the B6105. Back in the days of the railway there was a level crossing here to allow access over the road. Make your way across, but instead of continuing on the Longdendale Trail you should head down the slope and pick up the Pennine Way, which is signposted. At this point, you are heading down towards the reservoir and you will soon end up at the dam wall. When you get there, turn right and walk right along it, with the water being on your right.

When you reach the other side of the dam wall, there are some steps for you to climb up and you then need to look out for a path leading to the Pennine Way. At the top of the path, the Pennine Way branches off and you instead need to look out for the bridleway and footpath signed

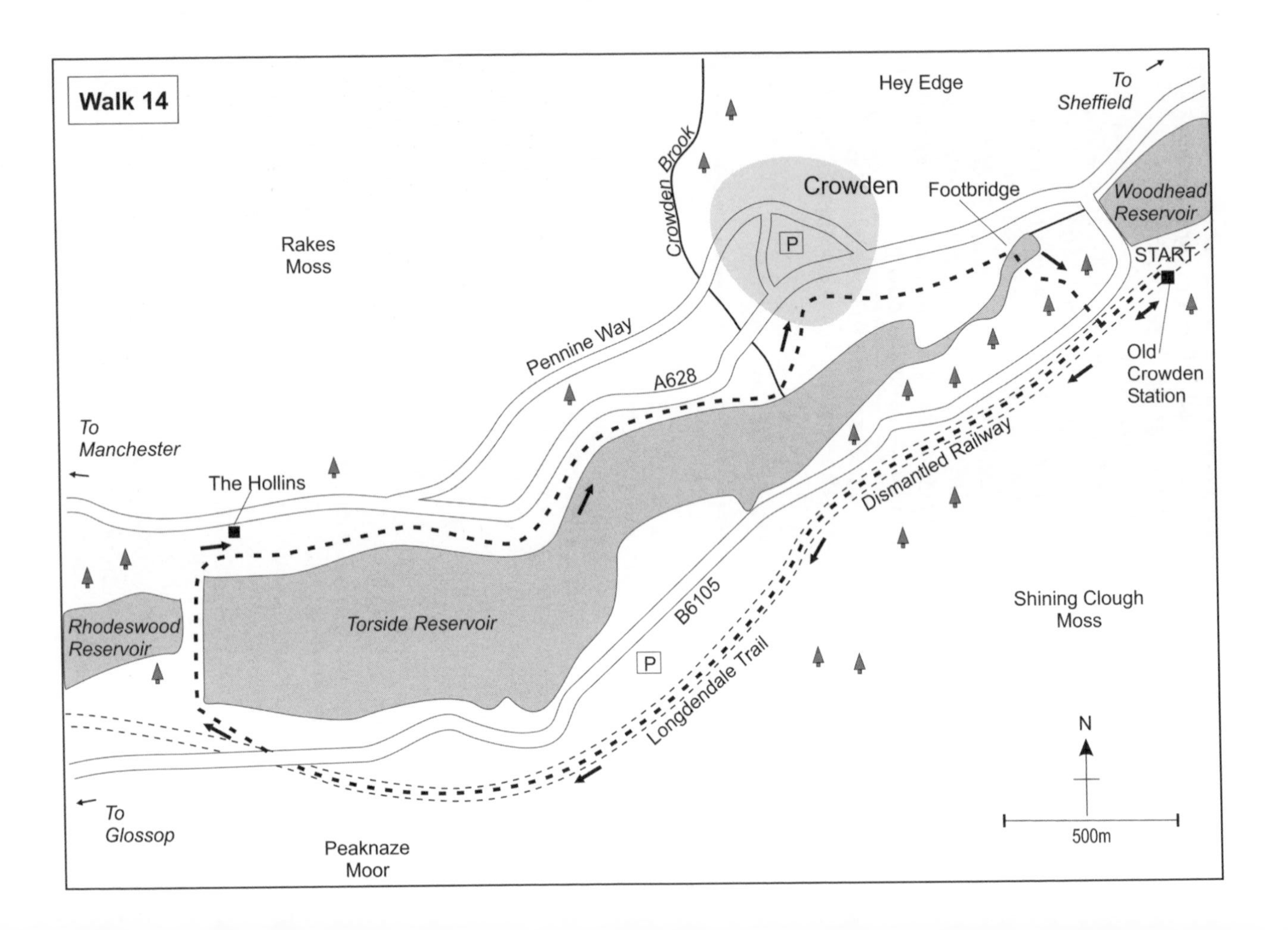

Walk 14
Hey Edge
To Sheffield
Crowden Brook
Crowden
P
Footbridge
Woodhead Reservoir
START
Rakes Moss
Pennine Way
A628
Old Crowden Station
To Manchester
The Hollins
Dismantled Railway
Rhodeswood Reservoir
Torside Reservoir
B6105
Shining Clough Moss
P
Longdendale Trail
N
To Glossop
500m
Peaknaze Moor

off to the right which heads into the trees. Go through a gate and then you see a sign pointing off to the right along Torside concessionary footpath. Go through the kissing gate here and continue along the path through Tinsel School Wood. You'll then have to cross over a little stream on a footbridge and climb over a stile. Head down the hill on the path, go through a kissing gate and cross over another little bridge, pretty much opposite the sailing club, before continuing to head straight on along the path at the side of the reservoir.

As you carry on along this path, it looks as though you are going to be brought out at the main road near Crowde, but no; there will be a footpath on your right signed for Woodhead Dam and you need to take this. Keep going towards the dam wall, climb the steps and go over the bridge to reach the other side of the valley. When you get to the other side, there is a track going up the hill to the right and you need to head up this, through the trees. At the top of the track you will be brought out at the A6105 road. Carefully cross it and look out for the signs marking the

Torside Reservoir

The route of the old line at the former Crowden Station

Longdendale Trail at the other side. You need to turn left onto it and head back to the starting point at the old Crowden Station. However, if you have parked at Torside Reservoir, you will need to turn right here and head back to the car park in the other direction.

Walk 15
Dunford Bridge

This walk starts close to the Woodhead Tunnel and along a section of the Trans Pennine Trail, the former line that once carried goods and passengers from one side of the hills to the other.

Woodhead Tunnel

There are three parallel tunnels that leave Dunford Bridge and come out at the other side of the hills at Woodhead, all of them referred to as The Woodhead Tunnel. The first tunnel was completed in 1845 and the second in 1852, both being opened to improve the rail link between Sheffield and Manchester. Both tunnels claimed the lives of several workers, due to the tough conditions and outbreaks of disease. But, once completed, these engineering feats through tough millstone grit were a remarkable achievement and the first tunnel was one of the longest in the world when

Woodhead tunnel *(photograph © Ben Brooksbank)*

its three mile route was finally dug out. The first two tunnels operated right up until the electrification of the line in 1953 when the third tunnel was built for this precise purpose. But despite a significant investment in the whole line, talk soon began of using the tunnel for other purposes in the 1960s, including a cross-Pennine motorway. With the other Pennine route doing well along the Hope Valley, declining passenger numbers meant that the Woodhead route was mothballed and the last passenger carriage disappeared into the Peak District hills during 1970. The line continued to be useful for freight trains, but became completely disused in 1981. The tunnels are now owned by National Grid and the first two have been used for some time to carry electrical cables. National Grid then began converting the third tunnel to carry cables, and this was ongoing as this book was written. The use of the third tunnel for this purpose was controversial and there were protests to the work starting, given that it would be much more difficult to convert the tunnel back to rail use in the future if the work went ahead.

Dunford Bridge Station

The line up to Dunford Bridge was complete before the Woodhead Tunnel was finished, so at first a stagecoach was provided to head over the hills and link up with the station at Woodhead. The official opening of the

Dunford Bridge in 1954 *(photograph © Ben Brooksbank)*

station came on July 14, 1845, and at that time there were two platforms with a stone building for the booking office and accommodation for the workers. When the line was electrified and became ready to speed through the new Woodhead Tunnel in the 1950s, a new station building had to be constructed on the realigned route. Despite the investment in electrification, there was a decline in trade during the 1960s and the station was eventually closed down on January 5, 1970.

While standing anywhere in Dunford Bridge, it's hard not to notice the huge dam wall that dominates the skyline to the west. Behind this is Winscar Reservoir, a body of water quenching the thirst of those living in Manchester and also providing a centre for water sports enthusiasts. The most popular building in Dunford Bridge used to be the local pub, called The Stanhope. But this establishment served its last pint in 2000 so you'll have to travel a little further for your post-walk reward.

Length	**6.6km/4.1miles**
Allow	**2 hours**
Terrain	**Good paths with some slight inclines in the second half of the walk. The first section is on the Trans Pennine Trail and a short distance is walked on a country road**
Refreshments	**The pub in Dunford Bridge is no longer open, but if you head for the Woodhead Pass and turn left you'll soon come to the Dog and Partridge that serves food and drink. Tel: 01226 379731 ww.dogandpartridgeinn.co.uk**
Getting there	**Head for the A628 Woodhead Pass and when you are half way between the junctions with the A616 and the A6024, you will see a sign pointing you towards Dunford Bridge and the Trans Pennine Trail. Head along here and you'll see the car park on the former site of the station in the centre of the hamlet. Grid reference SE 158, 024**
Next stations	**Back when the Woodhead Tunnel was operational, trains ran towards Manchester via Longdendale and to Penistone through Hazlehead Bridge**
Map	**OS Outdoor Leisure 01 Dark Peak Area**

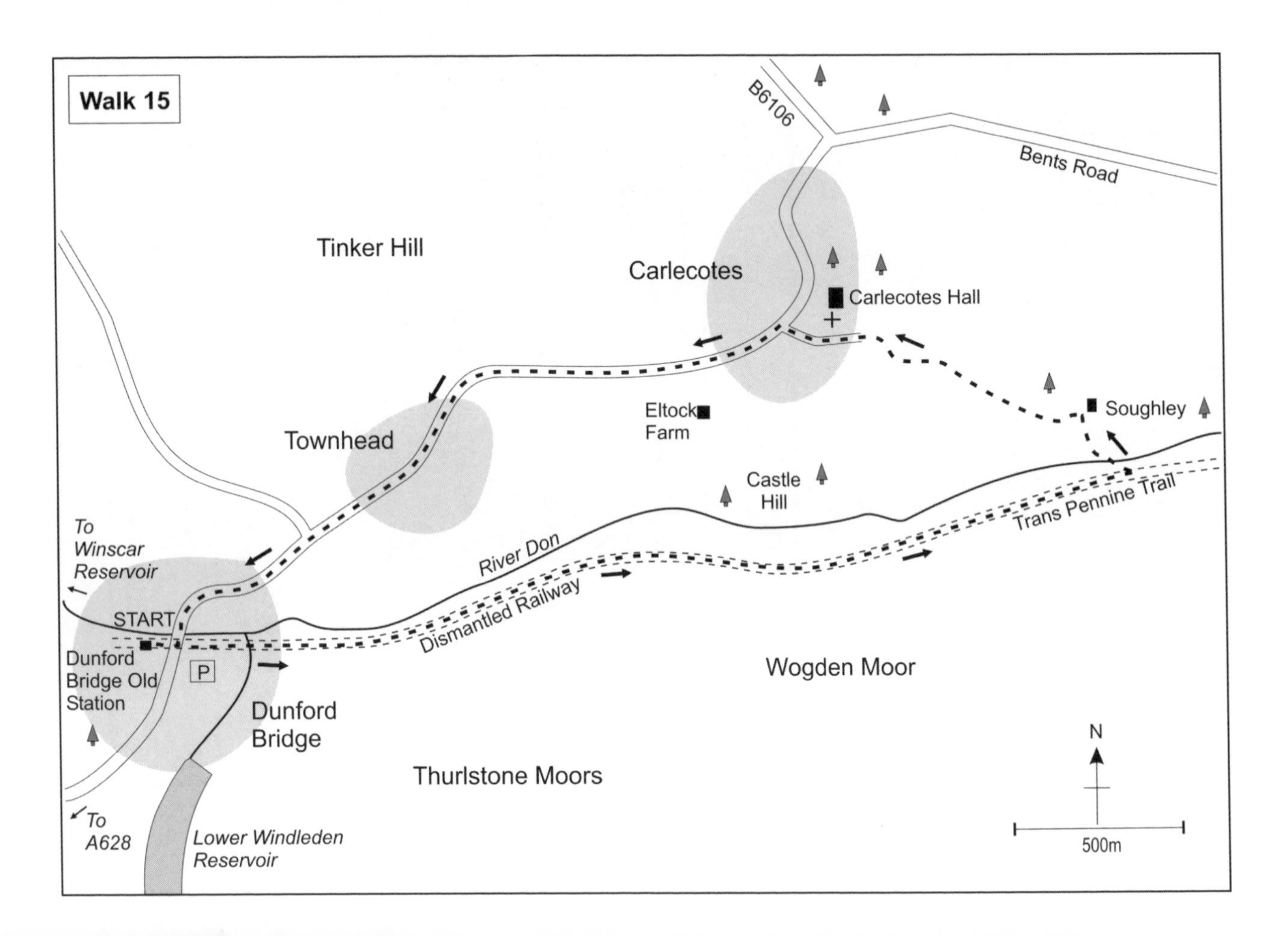
Walk 15
B6106
Bents Road
Tinker Hill
Carlecotes
Carlecotes Hall
Townhead
Eltock Farm
Soughley
Castle Hill
Trans Pennine Trail
River Don
Dismantled Railway
To Winscar Reservoir
START
Dunford Bridge Old Station
P
Dunford Bridge
Wogden Moor
Thurlstone Moors
To A628
Lower Windleden Reservoir
N
500m

Route

From the Trans Pennine Trail car park in the middle of Dunford Bridge, head onto the trail itself and follow the sign heading east for Penistone. This is a nice and easy, level track that is also popular amongst both cyclists and horse riders. It can get muddy after heavy rain, but is wide enough to avoid any serious puddles. After walking for 2km you'll see a wooden post declaring that it's just 7km to Penistone. We're not heading along the trail that far, but after a further kilometre there is another wooden marker. Just after this and slightly before the bridge, look out for a path off to the left. Go up the steps, over the stile and down the path. There is another stile at the bottom of this path, which you should head over before going across the bridge.

Head beyond the farm building and just after this the path branches off to the left. You'll soon come to a gate and then you enter the field and can spot a wind turbine poking up over the field to the right. Make your way to the far left hand corner of this field, where you climb a ladder to enter the next field and make your way over to the far left hand corner once more. Go over a stone stile into the next field and follow the track as it bends across to the right. At the end of this field, go up and over the ladder and take a left to follow the track round.

As the track bends around to the right, look out for a path off to the right which cuts out the farm. Go past the church on your right and come out at the road, where you need to turn left. Walk on the road for a short distance before taking a track down to the left indicated by a footpath sign. Just before this track reaches the last house there is a footpath sign off over the wall to the right. Enter the field and stick to the left side of it. Keep to this path as it crosses several more fields on its way towards Lower Town Head. When the path brings you out onto the road once more, turn left and make your way down the hill towards Dunford Bridge. You'll see the car park on your left when you reach the dip in the road.

Walk 16
Hazelhead Bridge

Head through wonderful woodland, along the Trans Pennine Trail and finally across farmland as you get a feel of the rural areas once serviced by steam trains on the edge of the Peak District.

Hazlehead Bridge Station

When the Woodhead Line was being planned, it had been the intention to position a station here, a convenient place for buses to connect to Huddersfield. There was, however, a problem with the roads that ran to the area and so the plan was shelved, with links to Huddersfield instead being provided from Dunford Bridge. Following the signing of a petition by the residents of surrounding villages, a Hazlehead Station was opened in May 1846 and, from the following August, the omnibus to Huddersfield ran to and from this spot. Standing right next to the bridge over Huddersfield Road, the layout of the station is fairly obvious to make out today, and this walk takes you by the old station and beyond, over the

Woodhead Line *(photograph © Ben Brooksbank)*

bridge which today houses the Trans Pennine Trail. The original station was one of the shortest lived railway ventures, closing just one year later in a cost cutting measure. But in 1850 it was re-opened and re-named Hazlehead Bridge, serving passengers in the area for 100 years before closure in 1950. Goods trains continued to stop here until 1964, from when the sound of squeaky railway breaks was silenced.

Length	**8.5km/5.3miles**
Allow	**3 hours**
Terrain	**Well used paths with good signage. Some walking along country roads for short distances, and the route crosses the Woodhead Pass**
Refreshments	**From the car park, drive towards Midhopestones where you'll find the popular Ye Olde Mustard Pot pub. Tel: 01226 761155. www.mustardpot.co.uk**
Getting there	**The car park is close to the Flouch Roundabout (named after a nearby pub), where the A628 meets the B6106 and the A616. From the roundabout, head towards Stocksbridge and soon after you will see a Yorkshire Water car park on the left where this walk begins. Grid reference SE 201,012**
Next stations	**When passengers could hop on board a train at Hazlehead Bridge the next stops were either Dunford Bridge heading west or Penistone heading east**
Map	**OS Outdoor Leisure 01 Dark Peak Area**

Route

From the car park, head down the little path at the far side, cross the A616 road and head into the woods on the track. A little further ahead, go straight on following the sign for Brook House Bridge. Soon after, continue directly ahead once more as you follow the sign for Swinden. Go through a gate and enter an area with grassy fields on your right and woods on your left. Go through another gate and, when the track bends round a little to the left you need to take the track turning off to the right. Very soon after, there is a path off to the right that you need to take.

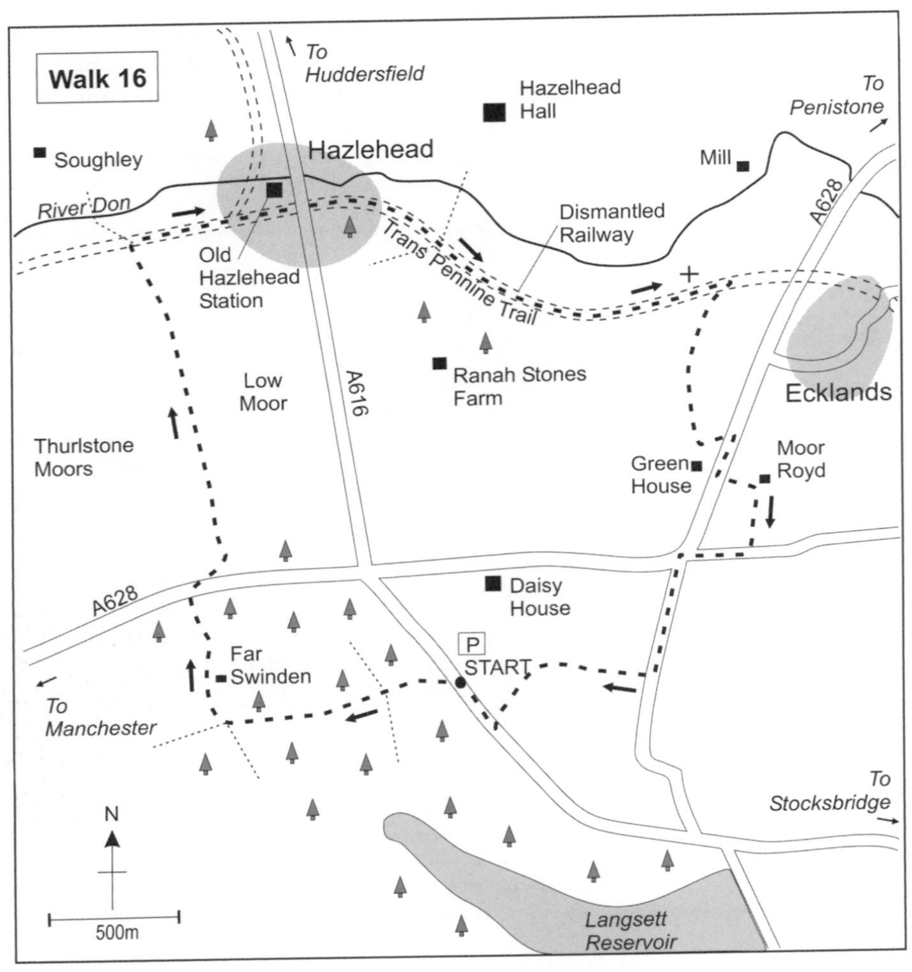

This path takes you across a field and, at the other side, you enter another wood. Follow the track straight ahead signed for the Trans Pennine Trail and continue right to the end of this track, passing the telephone mast and coming out at the Woodhead Pass A628 road. After carefully crossing the road, head for the footpath a little to the right. When you reach the two houses, turn left between them and follow the path straight ahead.

This is a long track, where good views open up. Look out for the wind farm on the right and three big wind turbines on the left. Go through a gate and carry on walking down to the end of the track. Go through another gate and follow the footpath sign to the left, which will take you down to the Trans Pennine Trail. Turn right onto the trail, making sure you are heading towards Hazlehead and Penistone. Walking along the Trans Pennine Trail, you go through Hazlehead Bridge Railway Station and across the footbridge over the B6106.

Continue on the trail, passing under a bridge and then on a stretch of the old railway track that now has silver birch trees on both sides. Soon after, look out for the settlement lagoon on the right that was developed to stop ochre pollution from the coal mines that used to operate in this area. When you reach Millhouse Green, turn left off the Trans Pennine Trail and then make a left turn on the road. You'll soon reach a gate on the left, which you should go through and continue across the old railway bridge.

As you enter the field, you can see a church on your right. Head for the far left corner of the field and go over the stiles to reach the second field, where you should go towards the house and take the path that runs up the left hand side of it. Follow the track out as it heads for the road, where you turn right. After walking a short distance along the road, take the track on the left. When you reach the houses, take the footpath on the right that goes through a garden and head out onto the field. On reaching the road at the far side, turn right onto it and this brings you to a junction, where you take the country road on your left.

The walk includes a section of the Trans Pennine Trail to Millhouse Green

Steadily climbing to the top of the hill, you can see the town of Stocksbridge on the left and Underbank Reservoir before it. Take the bridleway off the road to the right and follow this track all the way until it brings you out to the A616. To avoid walking the last section next to the busy road, cross over and enter the woods on the track opposite, a little to the right. Turn right onto the track that crosses your way, and soon after this junction take the right hand path again. Continue through the pine woodland before taking a right at the next junction of paths, and you will then be brought out at the A616 opposite the car park where the walk started.

Walk 17
Tissington

A short walk from one of the most gorgeous villages in the country, taking in part of the Tissington Trail and Limestone Way.

Tissington Station

As with many of the other stations on the Ashbourne Line, the buildings at Tissington were made of timber and so, unsurprisingly, there is nothing to show for them now. But the car park which forms the starting point for this walk and the site of the old station was in fact a popular destination for thousands of sightseers and hikers who loved this part of the country. That said, Tissington train station had a relative short-lived existence when compared to some of the other stations that have since closed in the Peak District. Opened in 1899, the close of this stop came in 1954 – well before the Beeching Axe started to wield its power. At least, it was in 1954 that scheduled passenger trains stopped dropping walkers off at Tissington; chartered trains continued until 1963 and were especially popular when the village's well dressing event was taking place.

Tissington Trail

The whole length of the 13 mile trail between Ashbourne and Parsley Hay was, of course, given its name by the village of Tissington. Derbyshire County Council and the Peak District National Park bought the route after the tracks were taken up in 1968. It was opened in 1971, just a few years after freight trains stopped using the route, and the Tissington Trail is now part of the National Cycle Network. As you may have experienced already, however, this route is not just for bikers. Walkers are in good supply here, horse riders make use of the fact it is also a bridleway and the good limestone base mean it is suitable for wheelchair users as well. The station building survives at Parsley Hay, the northern most point of the Tissington Trail, but there are plenty of other historic features along the way. Hartington signal box is a popular destination for walkers and cyclists alike, while an amble along the route will reveal bridges, signals and signage from the days of rail in the Derbyshire Dales. A walk along the Tissington Trail will give the impression that the former track bed is completely flat, but once you cover some distance on a bike it's a different story. Heading north from Ashbourne, through Tissington, to Parsley Hay, there is a very slight uphill gradient which makes for a much tougher route than for those heading south.

Ashbourne

The nearby picturesque town of Ashbourne, though just outside the National Park, is a place where many people head for when wanting a base to explore southern Derbyshire. It's proximity to some wonderful countryside and wide range of facilities make it a natural destination. Traffic can be busy here – it's the main route to Alton Towers – and the tourists help to clog the roads, but it's the start of the Tissington Trail and has good campsites and hotels, making it an asset for the region. A traditional market town, Ashbourne now has over 10,000 residents which call it home and the main business in the town is linked to tourism,

Length	2.5km/1.5 miles
Allow	45 minutes
Terrain	A short walk that is largely on the level and on well used paths and quiet country roads
Refreshments	Just after leaving the church yard at Tissington, the route passes Old Coach House tea rooms, serving drinks and meals. Tel: 01335 350501. There is also a refreshment kiosk at the station, open at peak times
Getting there	Best approached from the A515 that runs between Buxton and Ashbourne, the entrance to the village is through the rather grand Tissington Gates. This entrance is well signed off the A515, just follow the directions for Tissington. To reach the car park, head straight on, passing the candle workshop and the pond, and you will see the Tissington Trail car park on your right. This is the site of the old station. Grid reference SK 177, 520
Next stations	Tissington lay between Alsop to the north and Thorpe Cloud to the south
Map	OS Outdoor Leisure 24 White Peak Area

though this has not always been the case. Thanks to a rail link from the train station, Nestlé located a factory here in 1910 and made it the place where they created Carnation condensed milk. They made use of the dairy trains which could service their creamery and also distribute Derbyshire's milk to the south of England. When the milk trains stopped in 1965, milk

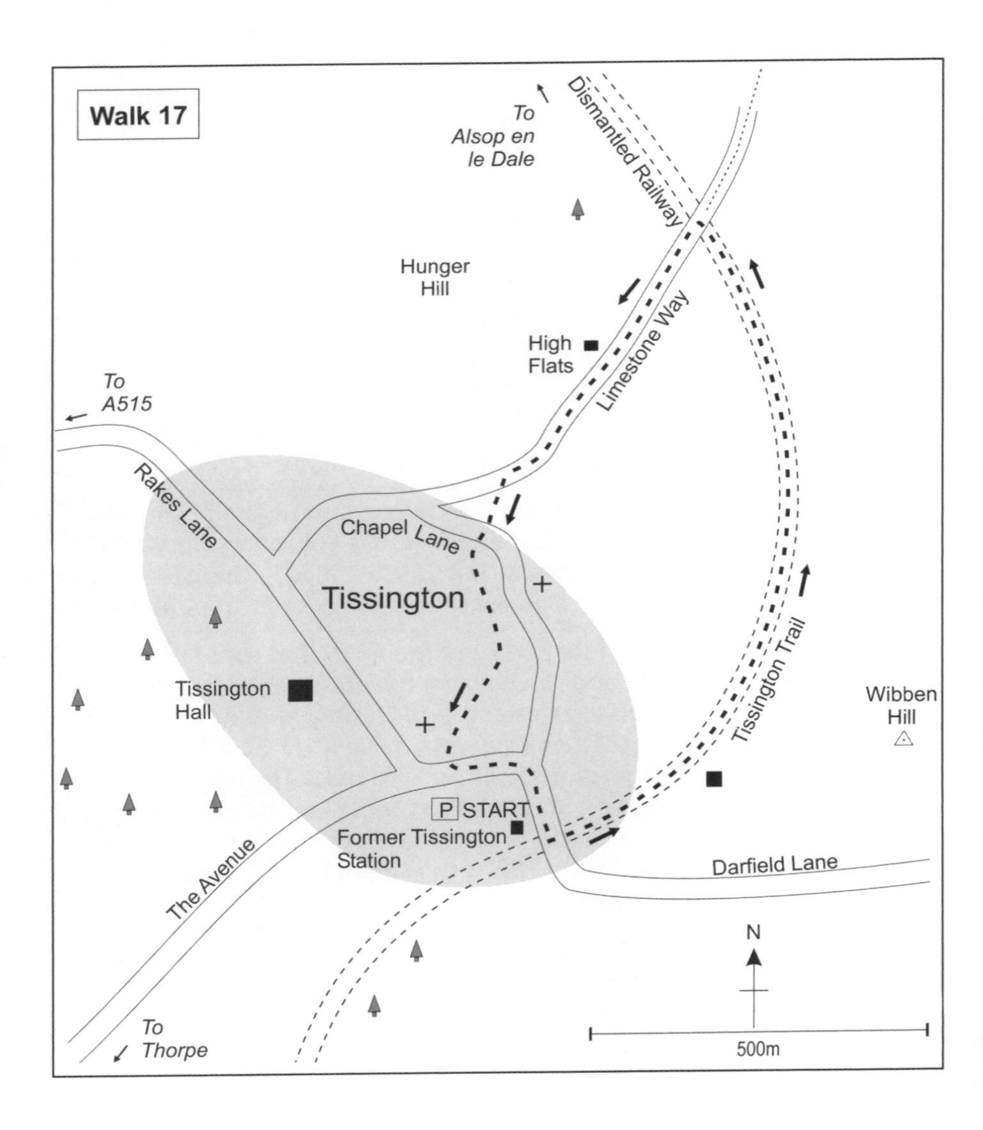

The church of Tissington is just one attraction of the picturesque village

was delivered to the factory by road until Nestlé closed the operation in 2003 with the loss of 100 jobs.

Route

From the car park at the site of the old Tissington train station, make your way to the cycle trail and follow it in the direction of Parsley Hay. Enter the railway cutting, which has steep slopes on either side, and then the track moves out of the trees at a left hand bend, opening up views of the surrounding countryside to the left and right. Just before you arrive at a bridge over the trail (grid reference SK 180, 529), take the path off to the left. On reaching the road at the top, turn left and you find yourself on the Limestone Way. After walking for some way on the track, take a footpath off to the left, keeping on the Limestone Way. Cross the field and then cross the road, taking the path across another field at the other side. Pass by the chapel on your left and head to the end of the field, where you go over a stile and move off to the right. Entering the church yard, continue to walk past the church and head down onto the road. Turn left onto the road, before turning left again at the junction. Go up this road, passing the pond on the right, and eventually you reach the car park at the old station site on the right.

You will see plenty of nosey sheep on your travels in the Peak District

Walk 18
Thorpe Cloud

Victorian tourists arrived by train to make the same hike you will do here, down fantastic Derbyshire Dales, passing tranquil streams and finding a rural peace among the limestone.

Thorpe Cloud Station

Despite being close to the village of Thorpe, the railway station took its name from the nearby hill, Thorpe Cloud. By giving it the name of the iconic landform which dominates the landscape in this part of the Peak District, this was sure to be a major destination for ramblers heading to the countryside from urban dwellings. Right from the opening in August 1899 this was a popular station for walkers to get off and explore one of the most beautiful areas of the country. Just a simple walk from the station brings you into outstanding scenery – a journey you are going to make by completing this route. Timetabled daily services stopped bringing tourists to Thorpe Cloud in November, 1954. But that was not the end of Thorpe Cloud's railway history. Special tourist passenger services and the movement of freight continued to operate until late 1963, when the final closure came. A year later the track was lifted and it lay disused until the Tissington Trail was formed.

Dovedale

A series of world class tourist attractions make Dovedale a brilliant place to explore, either as part of a day trip from the Tissington Trail or making the area a base for a longer stay. This has been a fashionable destination for centuries; the likes of John Ruskin, Lord Tennyson and Samuel Johnson all had favourable things to say about Dovedale, making it significant on an international scale. Today, it pulls in thousands of visitors – and a fair share of camera crews as well. More than one production of *Jane Eyre* has been filmed here, including Franco Zeffirelli's big screen version in 2006, and Russell Crowe's outing in *Robin Hood*. The main attraction is crossing the picturesque stepping stones to take a look at the fantastic limestone formations. There are a range of limestone spires that almost give the valley an Oriental flavour. They come with a range of unusual names, Twelve Apostles, Dovedale Church and

Lionshead Rock included, and the rocks are also littered with fossils. If you have trouble spotting them in situ in the rocks, keep an eye out as you cross the stepping stones, which are teaming with them. Whichever direction you approach Dovedale from and in whatever weather conditions you encounter on your visit, there is a charm and beauty which ensures most making the trek will arrange a return visit. And if you come in early November, you could experience one of the quirkiest sporting events in the UK. The Dovedale Dash, dating back to the 1950s, is a race from Ilam to Thorpe and a tough, cold slog it is too, at just under five miles across difficult terrain.

Length	**5.3km/3.3miles**
Allow	**2 hours**
Terrain	**Steep climbs and descents on this walk, sometimes taking place over rocky ground. Stepping stones need to be carefully crossed at Dovedale**

Victorians added the now iconic stepping stones and they have been photographed thousands of times

Refreshments	Dovedale is a great place to grab an ice cream and a drink, either from the kiosk near the stepping stones or by a slight deviation from this walk to the main Dovedale car park. The route also passes the Dog and Partridge pub in Thorpe, which serves meals at lunchtime and in the evening. Tel: 01335 350235 www.dog-and-partridge.co.uk
Getting there	Thorpe is a little village which lay between the A515 and A52 roads. From the A515, you need to head just to the north of Ashbourne and you'll see signs for Thorpe either at Tissington Gates or Mappleton. On the A52 heading out of Ashbourne to the west you'll see Ilam and Thorpe signed off to the right
Next stations	Tissington lay to the north and Ashbourne to the south
Map	OS Outdoor Leisure 24 White Peak Area

Route

Once settled at the car park, make your way to the road and walk along it until you reach the Dog and Partridge pub at the top. Cross over and take the road which goes to the right of the pub, passing a petrol station on the right. As you descend the hill, you can see the impressive Thorpe Cloud in front of you. At the bottom of the hill there is a hotel, but before you reach it take the footpath off to the right and cross the grass until your reach the National Trust sign indicating arrival at Thorpe Pastures.

From here, turn left on the footpath to Dovedale. Carry on along this path as it passes the hotel and follows the route of a wall, picking up a path heading to the right when you reach the end of this. The path bends to the right of the rocks and heads towards the hill in front of you, eventually bending left into Lin Dale. Keep an eye out for the rocks on the right of this path which are full of fossils; feel free to have a good look, but leave the rocks there for others to examine.

You will come out at Dovedale and see the famous stepping stones, which you need to cross. When you reach the other side, turn left onto the path. Continue on the path, with the river on your left. Before you reach the car park at the bottom, cross the bridge over the river. You may,

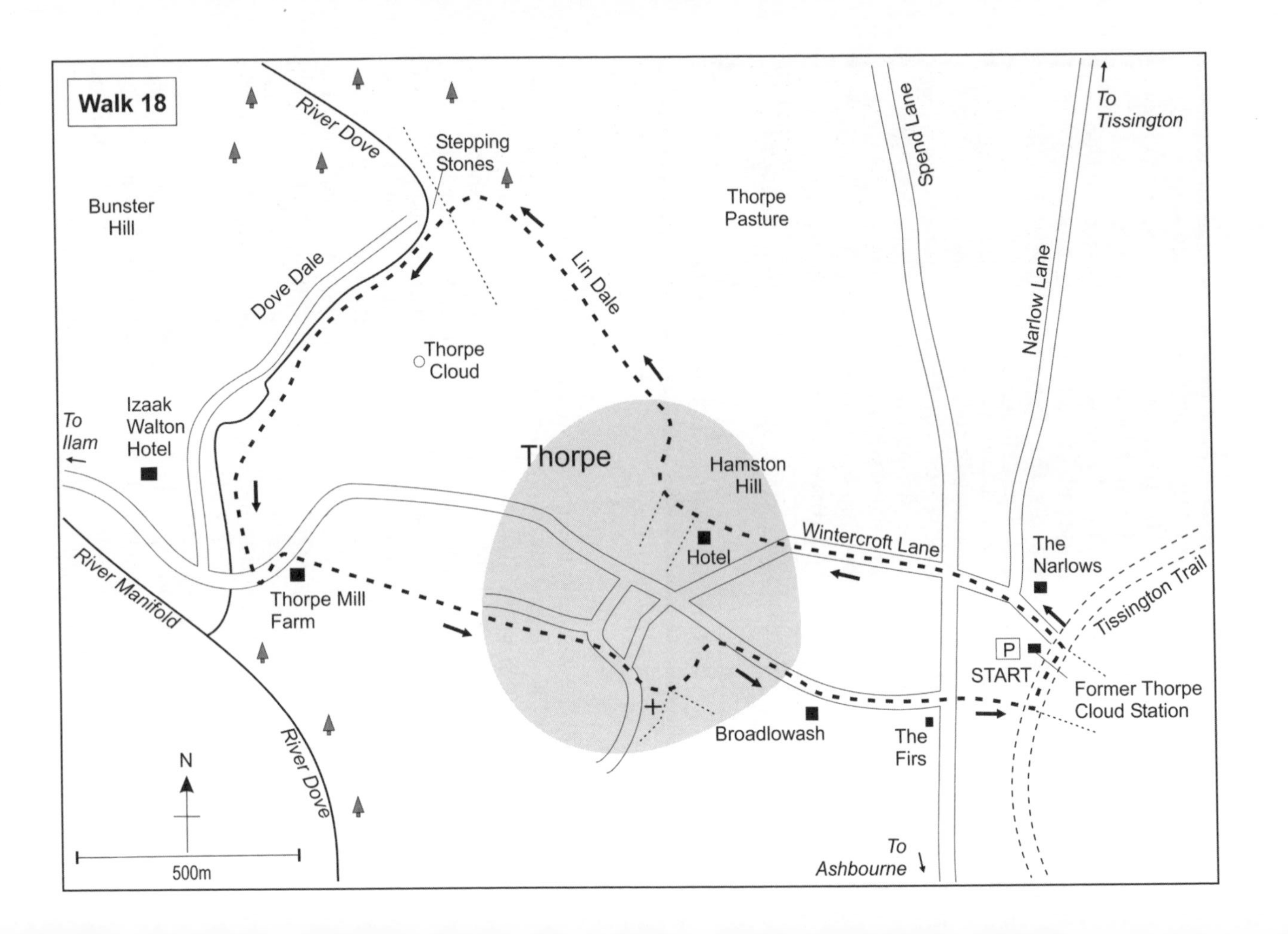
Walk 18
River Dove
Stepping Stones
Bunster Hill
Dove Dale
Lin Dale
Thorpe Pasture
Spend Lane
To Tissington
Narlow Lane
Thorpe Cloud
Izaak Walton Hotel
To Ilam
Thorpe
Hamston Hill
Hotel
Wintercroft Lane
The Narlows
Tissington Trail
River Manifold
Thorpe Mill Farm
P
START
Former Thorpe Cloud Station
Broadlowash
The Firs
N
River Dove
500m
To Ashbourne

Rural life in wonderful Dovedale

however, wish to make a diversion to the car park for an ice cream! Once you've crossed the bridge, take the footpath off to the right immediately at the other side. The path sticks close to the river and you'll have to pass through a couple of gates as you make your way over fields. When you arrive at the road, turn left onto it and head by Thorpe Mill Farm. Just after it, you will see two paths leading into the field, one branching to the left and one going straight on – you need the one that goes straight ahead, up the hill. After a steep climb, aim for the gate in the middle of the wall at the top, passing through it and going straight on.

You will soon see a barn ahead of you and the path continues on the left of it, leading to a track. Follow the track, but look out for the path next to a bungalow on the right that gives access to another field. Continue through a series of fields before arriving at a road in Thorpe, which you should turn right onto. Pass by Thorpe Village Hall and you'll soon see the church in front; take the path down to the left of it. When you pass the church, turn left onto the path you reach and when you reach the road turn right and head up the hill.

Once at the top of the hill, you pass a couple of barns at the top and then it levels out. Continue until you reach the main road. Take the footpath straight across, crossing a couple of field before rejoining the Tissington Trail. Turn left onto the track and you'll soon be back at Thorpe Station.

Walk 19
Alsop

The remote former station of Alsop provides us with a route into Alsop en le Dale, a charming little settlement which is all but hidden from the nearby A515.

Alsop Station

Although the busy A515 now sees cars constantly passing by the site of the former Alsop train station, it's not difficult to imagine the isolation of this stopping-point when it opened in the 19th century. The feeling of remoteness as the train chugged away and left silence in its wake must have been startling for city-dwellers who came here to explore the dales. Indeed, before the revolution of the train arrived, this corner of Derbyshire was even more isolated. By today's standards, it's inconceivable that a settlement the size of Alsop-en-le-Dale had a train station at all. Boasting only a handful of cottages and farms, Alsop-en-le-

Length	**2.2km/1.4miles**
Allow	**50 minutes**
Terrain	**A short, steep ascent at the end back to Alsop Station**
Refreshments	**None on the route itself, but head to Tissington village a little drive down the A515 where you will find the Old Coach House tea rooms. Tel 01335 350501**
Getting there	**On the A515 between Buxton and Ashbourne, Alsop-en-le-Dale is sandwiched between Hartington and Tissington. The turning for the car park at the former train station is well sign-posted and sits very close to the main road. Grid reference SK 155, 549**
Next stations	**Hartington lay to the north, while Tissington was once the next stop to the south**
Map	**OS Outdoor Leisure 24 White Peak Area**

Dale is also home to church dating back to Norman times and a rather grand looking hall, built for the Alsop family.

Route

Once you're at the car park at Alsop, head towards the bike trail and start walking towards Tissington. Just after going over the railway bridge there is a footpath on the left and you need to head down the steps. Once at the bottom, follow the footpath (number 325) towards Parwich Lees. Head for the far right corner of the first field before going through the gate into the second field, now heading for the far left corner where you will see a footpath sign by the trees. Take the path off to the left to Parwich

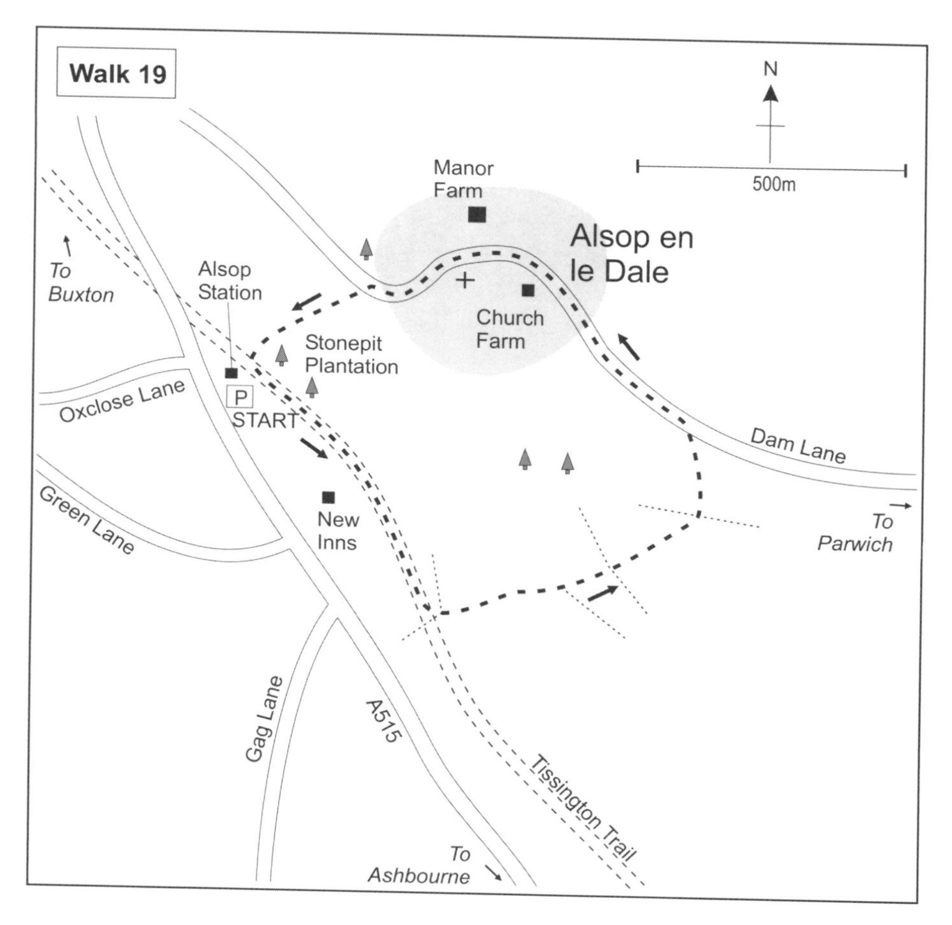

The approach back up to the Tissington Trail from Alsop en le Dale

Lees and head down to the far side aiming just to the right of the little wood. Go through the gap in the wall and follow the path straight ahead and slightly to the left towards Alsop, finding the track and taking it down to the left, where it brings you out at the road.

Turn left onto the road, called Dame Lane, heading into Alsop. Keep going into the village, passing the church on the left. The road bends down to the left and then, just as it bends to the right, there is a path you need to take on the left. This path goes up the hill and is the start of a fairly steep section of the walk. It follows the route of the dry stone wall and, as you approach the trees, the path switches to the other side of the wall. At this point you can see the Tissington Trail again. Continue on up, joining the trail and turning left to head back to the car park.

Walk 20
Hurdlow

The northern end of the High Peak Trail is the setting for a lovely round walk through limestone countryside and along a disused railway line that was once so important for local industry.

Hurdlow Station

First opening in 1833, the function of Hurdlow Station often changed in the 19th century to meet fashions and trends of the time. Primarily it was a goods station to serve the local limestone and farming industries, and this was the one and only purpose of building a stop at this point. In 1856, however, as the area became popular with tourists, the station started to take passengers and this continued until 1877 when the station closed entirely. This was not to be the end for Hurdlow, though. When the line

The wonderful High Peak Trail at its northern end

was extended to Ashbourne, the station was opened once more in 1894 for both goods and passengers. One of the most popular days for people to get off at Hurdlow was Easter Tuesday for the nearby Flagg Races, an annual tradition that started in 1892 and continues to this day. Timetables referred to the station as Hurdlow for Longor and Monyash, two popular villages for visitors. In the end, it was passenger services that survived longest here; the last goods train left the station in 1948. In 1954 the station was closed for the final time.

Length	**5.2km/3.2miles**
Allow	**1 hour 45 minutes**
Terrain	**Some gentle inclines**
Refreshments	**Close to the car park at Hurdlow you will find The Royal Oak pub, serving breakfasts and food throughout the day. Tel: 01298 83288 www.peakpub.co.uk**
Getting there	**Located on the A515 between Buxton and Ashbourne, the site of Hurdlow Train Station can be found to the west of Bakewell. Although it's not actually in Hurdlow, you will see the car park if you take the road signed to it, opposite the B5055. There is a pay and display car park at the train station, which is at grid reference SK 126, 659**
Next stations	**This station was sandwiched between Darlow Halt and Parsley Hay when it was in operation**
Map	**OS Outdoor Leisure 24 White Peak Area**

Route

The starting point for this walk is the former railway station at Hurdlow, now a car park for those enjoying the High Peak. Head north along the High Peak Trail towards Darlow, away from Parsley Hay, walking towards the end of the route. Following the route of the former railway station, look out first for the wonderful sight of the limestone walls that hem in the farming fields in this part of Derbyshire. The route then takes you through a limestone cutting and subsequently over an embankment as the engineers worked hard to keep the route level.

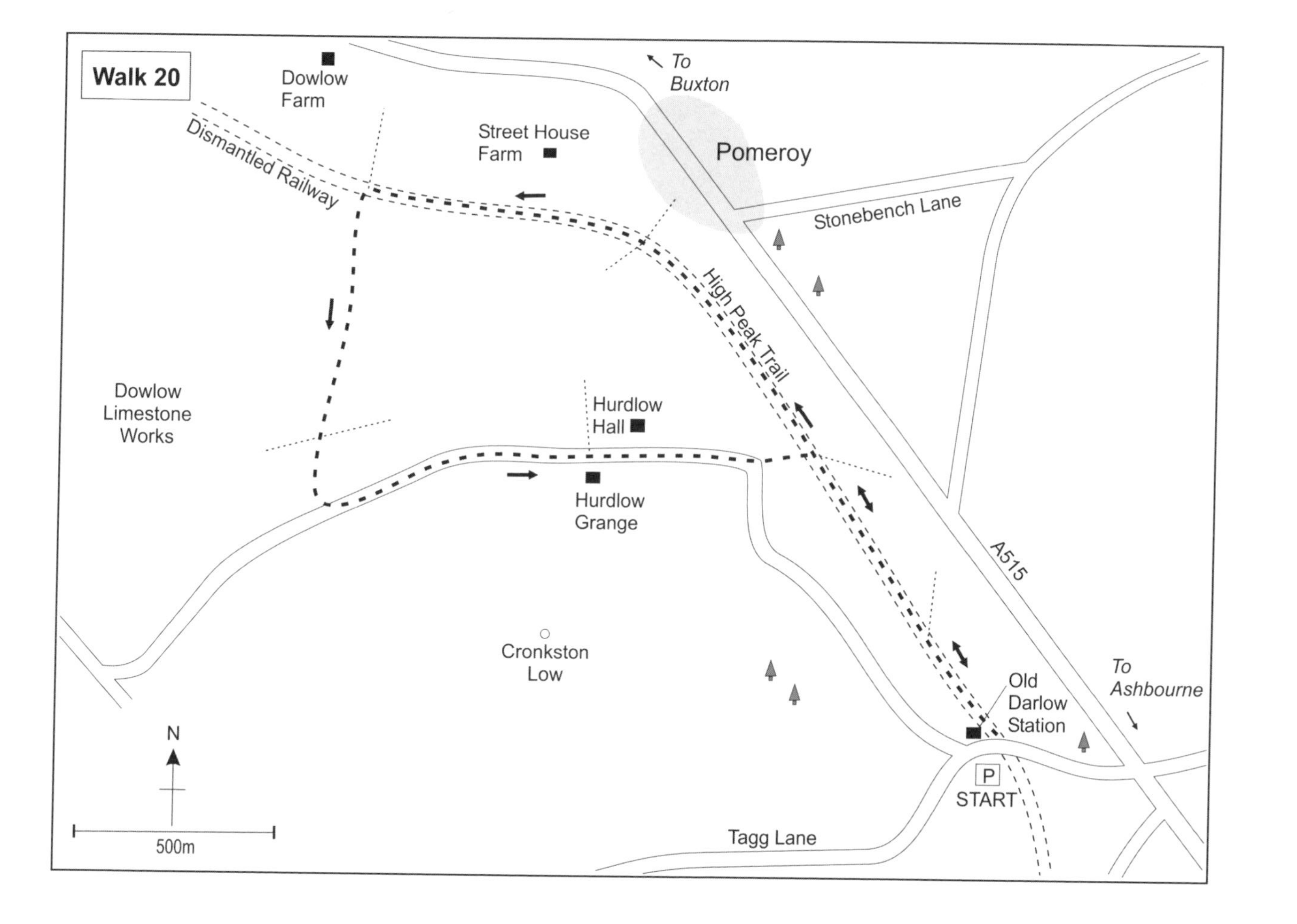

Walk 20
Dowlow Farm
To Buxton
Street House Farm
Pomeroy
Dismantled Railway
Stonebench Lane
High Peak Trail
Dowlow Limestone Works
Hurdlow Hall
Hurdlow Grange
A515
Cronkston Low
Old Darlow Station
To Ashbourne
P
START
N
Tagg Lane
500m

The former railway line is well used by walkers and cyclists

You need to head under a couple of bridges and pass a farm on the right as you come to the northern end of the High Peak Trail. At this point, at Darlow, you need to turn left on the track. Continue up the hill, and look out on the right for the vast area of limestone workings that have cut away this part of the Peak District. It has the double effect of being both disturbing in such a beautiful area but also strangely enchanting and interesting. Go up to the summit, where you can see High Wheeldon on the right with the trig point, and you come to a path on the left through a field, which you need to take.

At this point, there are great views all around and you need to aim for the far right hand side of the field, where you will see a stile and another footpath which takes you across another field. When you reach the track turn left and continue ahead, passing holiday cottages and a couple of farms at Hurdlow. When you approach a right hand bend in the road, take the footpath off to the left and head for the bridge across the field. Take the path off to the right which brings you back onto the High Peak Trail. Carry on along the trail and you will find yourself back at the car park where the walk started.